M marshall

from Grandma Kelly

DOG BREEDS

DOG BREEDS

AJ and HA Barker

GALLERY BOOKS
An Imprint of W. H. Smith Publishers Inc.
112 Madison Avenue
New York City 10016

Published by Gallery Books
A Division of W H Smith Publishers Inc.
112 Madison Avenue
New York, New York 10016

Produced by
Brompton Books Corp.
15 Sherwood Place
Greenwich, CT 06830
USA

Copyright © 1984 Brompton Books Corp.

Page 1 : West Highland White Terrier.
Page 2–3 : Rough Collie.
Page 4–5 : Bearded Collies.
Page 6–7 : The Smooth-coated and Rough-coated
Chihauhaus are the smallest breeds of dogs in the world.

All photographs kindly supplied by Animals Unlimited
excepting cover pictures and pages 2–3 which are
supplied by Panther Photographic International.

ISBN 0–8317–2406–4

Printed in Hong Kong

10 9 8 7 6 5 4

Contents

Classification of Breeds
There are about 400 breeds of dog in the world, just over 300 of which are registered and recognized by canine organizations. The American Kennel Club classifies the breeds into six groups: sporting breeds, hounds, working breeds, terriers, toys, and non-sporting breeds.

Sporting Group
American Water Spaniels
Brittany Spaniels
Chesapeake Bay
  Retrievers
Clumber Spaniels
Cocker Spaniels
Curly-coated Retrievers
English Cocker Spaniels
English Setters
English Springer Spaniels
Field Spaniels
Flat-coated Retrievers
German Short-haired
  Pointers
German Wire-haired
  Pointers
Golden Retrievers
Gordon Setters
Irish Setters
Irish Water Spaniels
Labrador Retrievers
Pointers
Sussex Spaniels
Vizslas
Weimaraners
Welsh Springer Spaniels
Wire-haired Pointing
  Griffons

Hound group
Afghan Hounds
American Foxhounds
Basenjis
Basset Hounds
Beagles
Black and Tan
  Coonhounds
Bloodhounds
Borzois
Dachshunds
English Foxhounds
Greyhounds
Harriers
Ibizan Hounds
Irish Wolfhounds
Norwegian Elkhounds
Otter Hounds
Rhodesian Ridgebacks
Salukis
Scottish Deerhounds
Whippets

Working group
Akitas
Alaskan Malamutes
Bearded Collies
Belgian Malinois
Belgian Sheepdogs
Belgian Terveuren
Bernese Mountain Dogs
Bouviers de Flandres
Boxers
Briards
Bullmastiffs
Collies
Dobermann Pinschers
German Shepherd Dogs
Giant Schnauzers
Great Danes
Great Pyrenees
Komondor
Kuvasz

Mastiffs
Newfoundlands
Old English Sheepdogs
Puli
Rottweilers
St. Bernards
Samoyeds
Shetland Sheepdogs
Siberian Huskies
Standard Schnauzers
Welsh Corgis, Cardigan
Welsh Corgis, Pembroke

Terrier group
Airedale Terriers
American Staffordshire
  Terriers
Australian Terriers
Bedlington Terriers
Border Terriers
Bull Terriers
Cairn Terriers
Dandie Dinmont
  Terriers
Fox Terriers
Irish Terriers
Kerry Blue Terriers
Lakeland Terriers
Manchester Terriers
Miniature Schnauzers
Norfolk Terriers
Norwich Terriers
Scottish Terriers
Sealyham Terriers
Skye Terriers
Soft-coated Wheaten
  Terriers
Staffordshire Bull Terriers
Welsh Terriers
West Highland White
  Terriers

Toy group
Affenpinschers
Brussels Griffons
Chihuahuas
English Toy Spaniels
Italian Greyhounds
Japanese Chin
Maltese
Manchester Terriers
Miniature Pinschers
Papillons
Pekingese
Pomeranians
Poodles (Toy)
Pugs
Shih Tzus
Silky Terriers
Yorkshire Terriers

Nonsporting group
Bichons Frisés
Boston Terriers
Bulldogs
Chow Chows
Dalmatians
French Bulldogs
Keeshonds
Lhasa Apsos
Poodles
Schipperkes
Tibetan Terriers

Introduction

Breeding dogs has become an art and a science. Every kind of dog for work, sport or amusement has been produced. With careful attention to lineage and conformation, and a certain degree of trial and error, many dog breeds have been tailor-made for different purposes — guard dogs, sheepdogs, hounds and pet dogs, to name a few. With increased knowledge of genetics and the great demand for a variety of dogs, breeders have steadily perfected the finer points and desirable qualities of each breed.

Within many types, inventive crossbreeding has engendered toy and miniature sizes; smooth-haired, wire-haired and long-haired varieties; and a wide and sometimes wild assortment of colors.

With its rich history and its colorful — if not sometimes startling — variety, the world of DOG BREEDS is as informative as it is fascinating.

Affenpinscher *Germany*

The Affenpinscher, which resembles a monkey, is a very old breed. It has always been regarded as a close relative of the more common smooth-haired Miniature Pinscher.

Its monkey-like appearance is due largely to its round, black, lustrous eyes. It is a sturdy little dog with a rounded skull, an undershot mouth, small pointed ears, a docked tail, and a wiry coat.

The color is generally black, but black with tan or gray markings is also found, as are other colors except very light ones.

Afghan Hound *Afghanistan*

The Afghan Hound is distinguished by its long silky coat, its springy gait, and aristocratic, albeit somewhat bizarre, bearing. It probably originated in the Middle East but subsequently became established in the rugged countryside of northern Afghanistan. There it was used for hunting. The Afghan's head is long, the jaws especially so, and the eyes are preferably dark. The coat is long and fine in texture, with a silky topknot on the head; the tail curls into a characteristic ring at the end. Afghans come in all shades of brown, in black, and black and brown, and they are extremely popular all over the world.

Above: Affenpinscher, originally bred in Germany as a ratting dog.
Left: Short-haired Afghan Hound.
Right: A very decorative and elegant looking Long-haired Afghan Hound.

Airedale Terrier *Britain*

Because of its large size the Airedale is unique within the terrier group. It is largely a descendant of the black and tan hunting terriers, now extinct, which were crossed with foxhounds in the Airedale Valley in Yorkshire.

The Airedale is a terrier in temperament and elegant in appearance. The head is long with a flat skull, flat cheeks, and very powerful jaws. The eyes are small, dark brown, and full of terrier expression in combination with calm confidence. The coat is hard and wiry with a soft undercoat. Left untended for too long, Airedales rapidly grow into woolly bears. The ears are small and folded, and carried to the side of the head.

The color on the head and legs is a warm tan, with black or dark grizzle on the rest of the body. Dogs stand about 23 inches at the shoulder, slightly less for bitches. The weight is usually around 55 pounds.

Akita *Japan*

The Akita, sometimes known as the large or Shishi Inu, is the biggest and one of the best known of the Japanese breeds. It comes from the Polar regions and was bred for hunting deer and wild boar. In former times it could be owned only by Japanese nobility. Today it is gaining favor in the United States where there are several specialist Akita breeders. The Akita loves to work, but also makes a good, gentle pet.

The Akita is swift, and with its webbed feet is a powerful swimmer. Its double coat and soft mouth enable it to retrieve even in the coldest waters. The top coat is medium to soft and straight; the undercoat thick and furry. It is large, compact and muscular with a fairly short neck, straight back and sturdy straight legs. The tail is curled and carried over the back. Colors are fawn, wheaten gray, brindle, russet, tan or black and tan, and all white. The height at the shoulder is 21 to 24 inches for dogs, and 19 to 21 inches for bitches.

Alaskan Malamute *Alaska*

The Alaskan Malamute is one of the Arctic spitz breeds named after the Eskimo group which is supposed to have developed the breed. It was used originally as a sledge dog by the Alaskans, and it is in fact the largest of the sledge-dog breeds.

The Alaskan Malamute is a big, powerful, energetic dog which carries its head proudly. The eyes are set obliquely and resemble those of a wolf, but having a friendly expression. The coat is thick and coarse, particularly abundant on the chest, neck, and tail, where it forms a plume.

The color is usually gray or black with white marking. Dogs stand 25 to 28 inches at the shoulder, bitches 23 to 25 inches.

Right: Airedale Terrier.
Inset: Alaskan Malamute.

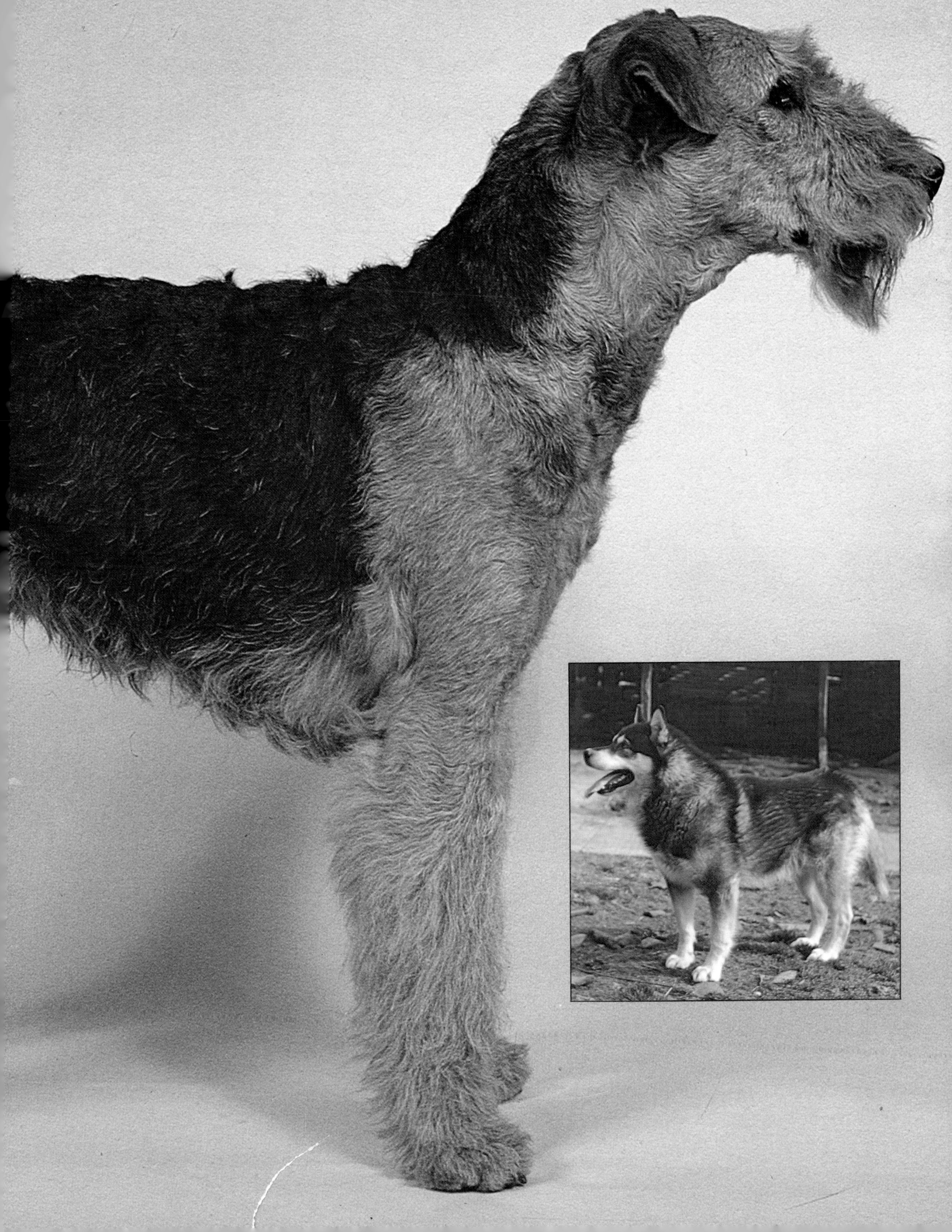

American Coonhound *USA*

This black and tan Coonhound is the only one of the six varieties of Coonhound officially recognized as a breed by the American Kennel Club. It is used primarily for hunting raccoon and opossum. As distinct from the other Coonhounds, it is a close relative of the English Bloodhound, though it also has unmistakable traces of the American Foxhound. Although it resembles a Bloodhound, the American Coonhound is of lighter build and it lacks the folds of loose skin on the forehead. The ears are low set, long, and pendulous.

American Foxhound *USA*

The main difference between the American Foxhound and its English counterpart is its size, for it is generally a much bigger and longer-legged dog. The ears are large, the body is strong and well built, and the tail is carried straight up. All colors are acceptable. Height at the shoulder is usually just over 24 inches.

American Staffordshire Terrier *USA*

The American Staffordshire Terrier, which should not be confused with the Staffordshire Bull Terrier, is a wholly American breed. It is related to the Staffordshire Bull Terrier in that both breeds had a common origin in Bulldog and terrier crosses. The American dog is taller, however, and generally looks more like a true terrier than the Staffordshire Bull. Originally it was bred for fighting and around 1900 was known as the 'American Pit Bull Terrier' or 'Yankee Terrier'; only since 1936, when the breed was recognized by the American Kennel Club, has it been known as the American Staffordshire Terrier.

The American Staffordshire Terrier has a deep head of medium length, with a moderate muzzle and very pronounced cheek muscles. The eyes should be dark and round. For show purposes the ears are erect and cropped; if uncropped they should be 'rose' or pricked, but never dropped. The front legs are set wide apart to permit a powerful chest; the hindquarters are powerfully muscled and the feet are compact. The tail is short and set on low. The breed comes in all colors; the height is 17 to 19 inches.

American Toy Terrier *USA*

The American Toy Terrier is not officially recognized as a separate breed. Despite this, it is very popular as a pet. It is descended from the Fox Terrier but its forebears incorporated various toy breeds.

The American Toy Terrier resembles a small Smooth Fox Terrier but is much finer in bone and has pricked ears. The head is more pointed and the jaws weaker. The erect tail is docked.

The color is usually white, with black or black and tan markings. A typical example should not exceed 8 to 9 pounds in weight.

American Water Spaniel *USA*

The American relative of the Irish Water Spaniel is considerably smaller than its ancestor. It is, however, slightly longer in body and has a broader skull. The coat is tightly curled.

The color is liver or chocolate brown; small white markings on the toes and chest are acceptable. Height at the shoulder is 15 to 18 inches.

Australian Cattle Dog *Australia*

The Australian Cattle Dog is considered to be a cross between the Collie, Kelpie, and Dingo. Be that as it may, the fact that the breed earns its keep herding cattle is beyond doubt.

The Australian Cattle Dog is light, agile, and active. The head is broad with a slightly domed skull and gradually tapering foreface. The ears are pointed, carried erect at a slight angle. The eyes are dark and oval. The nose is black. The body is of moderate length and strongly built. The front legs are straight with slightly sloping pasterns; hindquarters have hocks well let down. The tail reaches the hock, is well covered with hair and carried in a gentle upward curve. The coat is fairly short and rough with a soft, thick undercoat.

The color is usually a mottled blue with or without black markings. The head is blue or black and tan, and the tan should extend to markings on the forelegs, brisket, and on the inside of the thighs. The color may also be red speckled with rich red markings on the head. Height at the shoulder is about 18 inches.

Australian Kelpie *Australia*

The Kelpie is the Australian sheepdog, descended from short-haired, prick-eared Scottish sheepdogs which were sent to Australia about 1870. It is considered to have exceptional qualities of scent, sight, and hearing, and plays a key role on Australia's vast sheep-rearing stations. One well-trained Kelpie, it is said, can do the work of six men.

The Kelpie is a clean-cut, tough, and muscular dog with a fox-like head. The stop is well defined; the eyes are almond-shaped and may be light or dark according to the color of the coat. The ears are set wide apart and carried erect at a slight angle. The neck is clearly arched. The body is lithe, the back of moderate length giving a rectangular outline. It is not too heavy in bone, the feet are well knuckled up with hard pads and strong nails. The tail is bushy and is carried low in repose or high in action. The coat is short, straight, thick, and feels rough to the touch.

The color may be black, black and tan, red, red and tan, fawn, chocolate, or smoke blue. Dogs stand about 18 to 20 inches at the shoulder.

Australian Terrier *Australia*
Before World War II Australian immigrants
came mostly from the United Kingdom and they
took their terriers with them. These dogs, all
different varieties, eventually produced the
conglomerate out of which the Australian
Terrier breed was born.

The Australian Terrier is a rather low-set,
active little dog, with a keen expression in its
dark eyes. The ears are small, pricked, or
dropped forward. The neck has a decided frill of
longer hair.

The color is dark blue or silver gray with rich
tan markings on the head and the legs. Height
at the shoulder is about 10 inches and the
weight about 12 to 14 pounds.

Below: Australian Terrier.
Inset: Australian Cattle Dog.

Basenji *Central Africa*

The Basenji is an unusual – some say unique – member of the spitz breeds. Although they are comparatively new to the Western world, Basenjis have long been known in Central Africa, where they are used mainly for hunting and tracking game.

The Basenji cannot bark and the only noise it can make is a chortling yodel. Its other distinguishing feature is its cleanliness; to clean itself a Basenji behaves almost like a cat.

The Basenji is a lively and graceful animal, finely boned. The head is characterized by dark eyes, wrinkled forehead and pointed ears. The tail is set high and tightly curled close to the thigh. The skin is very supple, the coat sleek and close.

The color is usually pure chestnut and white, but sometimes tricolor. The height at the shoulder for dogs is about 17 inches, and about 16 inches for bitches. The weight is around 20 pounds.

Basset Hound *Britain*

With its Bloodhound-type head on a short-legged, long and heavily built body, and its long tail, the Basset Hound presents a stolid, some-what bizarre appearance. But it has a gentle temperament and has become a popular pet.

The Basset was used originally in France and Belgium for hunting. Its most prominent characteristics are a soulful expression, loose skin, and long, low shape. The coat is smooth and short.

Any recognized hound color is acceptable, but generally it is tricolor (black, white, and tan) or lemon and white. The height at the shoulder is about 20 inches and weight about 44 pounds.

Beagle *Britain*

Compared with the Foxhound, which is rarely seen at the dog shows these days, the rise in popularity of the Beagle has been meteoric and universal. Yet the Beagle has much in common with the Foxhound, which, like the Beagle, is a hunting dog. The Beagle is sturdy and of a compact build, giving the impression of great stamina and energy. The head is powerful without being coarse, the skull domed with a well-defined stop (the angle between the forehead and the muzzle), the nose broad, and the ears long and fine in texture. The neck is moderately long, well set into a noticeably ribbed, muscular body. The legs are straight, of good substance, round in bone, and with well-knuckled, strongly padded feet. The tail is carried gaily but not curled over the back. As well as the smooth-coated Beagle, which has a short and very close coat, there is also a less common rough-coated variety, which has dense wiry hair.

The color varies, but any recognized hound color — which usually includes some white — is acceptable. The height at the shoulder is 12 to 16 inches.

Left: Basenji.
Inset left: Basset Hound.
Inset far left: Beagle.

Bearded Collie *Britain*

All Collies hail from Scotland. Bearded Collies were known before the twentieth century as the Highland Collie, when they were purely working dogs in the Scottish Highlands. Nowadays they are more often the glamorous pets of the fashionable set. The Bearded Collie is active and strongly built without the massive appearance of the Old English Sheepdog and, above all, without the enormous coat of the latter. The coat is profuse and shaggy without being too thick, and is particularly abundant around the eyes and foreface.

The color is slate or sandy with or without white. The height at the shoulder is 20 to 24 inches for dogs, 18 to 22 inches for bitches.

Below: A Bearded Collie. This type of Collie was originally bred in Scotland as a working dog, but is now kept as a pet. Right: Bedlington Terrier.

Bedlington Terrier *Britain*

The Bedlington is essentially a wholly British terrier. Opinions differ as to whether the Dandie Dinmont contributed to the development of the Bedlington breed or vice versa, but the early specimens of both breeds are said to have had much in common.

When the old Bedlington was crossed with the Whippet, the outline of the original breed changed, the stubby legs becoming longer and the frame taking on a more streamlined look. The result combined the merits of terrier and hound coupled with a pleasant disposition.

The Bedlington is a graceful dog with a pear-shaped head. The head and skull are narrow, the jaw long and tapering with no stop. The nose should be black for blues and tans, brown for livers and sandy colors, with small, bright eyes — dark for blues, light for livers and sandies. The tail should be thick, tapering, and gracefully curved. The height for dogs is 16 inches, bitches 15 inches. The weight is 17 to 25 pounds.

Belgian Malinois *Belgium*
The Belgian Malinois, which takes its name from the town of Malines, is a variety of Belgian sheepdog. The main difference between this dog and its two relatives, the Tervueren and the Groenendael, is the coat and, in the latter case, the color. The Malinois is of the same type as its relatives; the texture of its coat is, however, much more like that of a German Shepherd. All three varieties of Belgian Sheepdog have the same marked aversion to moving in a straight line and instead tend to move in circles.

The Malinois and the Tervueren are the same color; the coat varies from fawn to mahogany with black tips, slightly lighter on the dog's underside. White is only acceptable on the toes, as is a small white spot on the chest. The height at the shoulder is 24 to 26 inches for dogs, 22 to 24 inches for bitches.

Belgian Sheepdog *Belgium*
An important variety of Belgian Sheepdog is the Groenendael, which looks rather like a black German Shepherd although it has a slightly lighter and taller build.

Like the Malinois and the Tervueren, the Groenendael is a herding breed. It was not until the turn of the century, however, that the classification was introduced which made them into breeds in the modern sense. The Belgian police force has used Groenendaels for many years, but elsewhere they are kept primarily as companions and pets.

The Groenendael has an alert and attentive expression, a pointed foreface, and eyes which vary in color from amber to brown. Its coat forms a mane round the neck and its tail is bushy. The color is black. The height at the shoulder is 24 to 26 inches for dogs, 22 to 24 inches for bitches.

Belgian Tervueren *Belgium*
The characteristics and appearance of the Belgian Tervueren are very similar to those of the Belgian Sheepdog. Like the Groenendael, to which it is closely related, the Tervueren resembles a light, lanky German Shepherd although there is little trace of that breed in its pedigree.

The breed differs from the Groenendael chiefly in color – brown with black tips to the coat. The height at the shoulder is 24 to 26 inches for dogs, 22 to 25 inches for bitches.

Both breeds, which are fairly rare outside Belgium, take their names from the Belgian villages near Brussels from which they are thought to have originated.

Bernese Mountain Dog *Switzerland*
The Bernese Mountain Dog was hardly known outside Switzerland until quite recently and it has now exchanged the role of sheepdog for family pet. It bears an unmistakable resemb-

lance to the St. Bernard.

In size and general outline the Bernese Mountain Dog is not unlike the Golden Retriever. It is a strong and agile dog, with a broad head, dark brown eyes, and ears carried close to the head. The coat is profuse, close, and fairly soft.

The color is black with smaller tan markings on the foreface and legs, a white blaze on the head, and a white 'shirt front.' The height at the shoulder is 25 to 28 inches for dogs, 23 to 26 inches for bitches.

Bichon Frisé *France*
The name Bichon (literally lap dog) has often been used to describe a family of small, usually white dogs to which the Belgian Bichon, the Maltese, the Teneriffe Dog, and the Bichon Frisé belong. In recent years the latter has become especially popular.

It is not unlike the Maltese but its curly, silky hair is more profuse, especially on the head. The color of the Bichon Frisé is white or white with apricot or dark gray patches on the ears and body. The height at the shoulder should be between 8 and 12 inches.

Bloodhound *Britain*
The Bloodhound is now regarded as a pure British breed since it has been mostly used and appreciated by Britain for centuries, but its original forebears were French. Nowadays it is kept primarily as a wrinkled and good-humored pet but, because of its sensitive nose and ability to follow a trail, it is sometimes used as a tracker dog.

The Bloodhound is a large, powerful animal with a dignified expression. Its skin is loose and baggy, the head long and narrow with long, thin, pendulous ears. The coat is short and usually black and/or tan. The average height at the shoulder for dogs is 26 inches, 24 inches for bitches. The weight should be at least 90 pounds and 80 pounds each.

Above: Groenendael.
Inset above right: Bernese Mountain Dog.
Inset below right: Bloodhounds.
Right: Border Terrier.

Border Collie *Britain*
The Border Collie is not officially recognized as a breed. It resembles a small and very much less refined version of the Rough Collie; the head is broader and coarser, the ears not as elegantly set and carried, and the coat is not as profuse.

The color is usually black with white markings, and the height at the shoulder is about 18 to 20 inches.

Border Terrier *Britain*
Like the Border Collie, the tough little Border Terrier originated in the Cheviot Hills bordering on Scotland. It was bred as a working terrier to hunt foxes which preyed on the sheep in that region. Nowadays most Border Terriers are kept as suburban pets, a role for which they are ideally suited because they are small, clean, adaptable, loyal, and gentle with children.

The Border Terrier is an active and hardy little dog with a dense and somewhat harsh coat. The head is shaped like that of an otter, the eyes dark, the ears small. Color varies — red, sandy, sandy and tan, or blue and tan. The weight for dogs varies between 13 and $15\frac{1}{2}$ pounds, bitches between $11\frac{1}{2}$ and 14 pounds. The height at the shoulder is 11 to 14 inches.

Inset left: Borzoi.
Below: Boston Terrier.
Right: Boxer.
Inset right: Bouvier de Flanders.

Borzoi *USSR*

The Borzoi is one of the traditional beauties of the canine world. It came to the West from the USSR and was known as the Russian Wolfhound. Before the Revolution the aristocracy of the Russian Imperial Court kept teams of Borzois for the traditional sport of hunting the wolf. Despite this background, the Borzoi has a friendly temperament. It is a graceful dog with great muscular power and speed; the head is of classical mold, long, lean, and narrow with almond-shaped eyes. The body is rather narrow but with great depth of brisket, the back rising in a graceful arch and covered in a long, silky, flat, or curly coat. The long, elegant tail has profuse and soft feathering.

All colors are acceptable. The height at the shoulder for dogs is from 29 inches, bitches from 27 inches.

Boston Terrier *USA*

The jaunty little Boston Terrier is recommended as a pet, especially for families with children; few breeds are so easy to manage and such pleasant companions. Yet the Boston Terrier descends from fighting dogs.

Originally, Bulldogs and terriers were used for dogfights, but when someone hit on the idea of combining the strength of the Bulldog with the tenacity of the terrier, the forerunner of the Boston Terrier breed was born.

Since then breeders have reduced its size and made it a delightful companion without extinguishing the terrier spark. It has spread and gained popularity nearly all over the world.

Although the Boston Terrier is one of the smaller breeds, it does not give the impression of being a toy dog; its compact body and stylish deportment demonstrate that it is determined, strong, and active.

Brindle and white is the most desirable color, but black and white is acceptable. The distribution of the white markings is usually considered of great importance: ideally there is a white blaze over the head, white muzzle, neck, chest, forelegs, and hind legs below the hocks. The height at the shoulder should not exceed 16 inches.

Bouvier de Flanders *Belgium*

A Bouvier always attracts attention — it is rare, it is of considerable size, and its appearance is distinguished. It is not unlike the Giant Schnauzer, but is even heavier and bigger boned. Like the Groenendael and the Tervueren, the Bouvier comes from Belgium where it was used for herding cattle.

The Bouvier is robust and thick set. The coat is double with a thick, soft undercoat and a harsh top coat, particularly abundant on the head where it forms moustaches, chin whiskers, and eyebrows which, according to the breed standard, gives the dog an unkempt look.

The color may vary from pale fawn to dark gray, sometimes black and red parti-color. The height at the shoulder is about 26 inches and weight 66 pounds.

Boxer *Germany*

The Boxer is a popular pet. Usually outclassed by the German Shepherd as a working dog, it is friendly, fond of children, and much more playful than its somewhat 'puzzled' expression would suggest.

It has, of course, a great deal in common with the Bulldog. In ancient Greece bull breeds were used as fighting dogs, but toward the end of the nineteenth century, the Boxer evolved into a type clearly distinguishable from a Bulldog.

The Boxer is muscular and clean cut. The shape of the head is its most important characteristic; the muzzle should be well developed, broad and square with a slightly underhung lower jaw. The coat should be short and shiny.

The color is brindle, red, or pied with a dark mask round the eyes and muzzle. Dogs stand 22 to 25 inches at the shoulder, bitches 21 to 23 inches.

Briard *France*

The Briard is descended from sheepdogs which accompanied the Asian armies that invaded Europe after the fall of the Roman Empire.

The Briard is tall with a long and shaggy coat. The head has a marked stop and the ears are cropped and heavily fringed. The long tail is carried low, the fringes forming a plume.

All colors are acceptable, but a dark, blackish gray is usually preferred. The height at the shoulder is 24 to 27 inches for dogs, 22 to 25 inches for bitches.

Brittany Spaniel *France*

The Brittany Spaniel is the only spaniel in the world that 'points.' They are very agile sprinters, adaptable and capable of great endurance.

The Brittany Spaniel is related to the old types of working spaniel which were imported into France from Great Britain. It is symmetrically built and on the same lines as modern English spaniels. The head is fairly broad, the ears are higher set than those of a Cocker Spaniel, and it is shorter in neck but longer in body and higher on the leg. The tail is short or nonexistent. The coat is thick and soft, but not too profuse except on ears, belly, and breeches where it forms attractive fringes.

The color is white with dark orange markings. The height at the shoulder is about 20 inches.

Brussels Griffon *Belgium*

The Brussels Griffon has two varieties: the Rough and Smooth coat. Its ancestry is very mixed, but the breed probably started off as a variation of the now fairly rare breed of German Affenpinscher farm dog. Initially kept as ratters, their self-assertiveness and determination to be with their owners at all times led them to a position in society as fashionable pets. Once established as such, other breeds were brought in to 'smarten' them up; these appear to have included a variety of terriers, pugs and — judging by the Brussels Griffon's large, expressive eyes — toy spaniels.

The Griffon Bruxellois is a compact, sturdy, and lively dog with an alert and cheeky expression. The head is large with a short, wide muzzle and a slightly undershot mouth, without showing the teeth or tongue. The eyes are large and dark, the ears very small and semierect. The coat is rough and straight, forming an abundant beard on the chin.

The color is either red, black, or black and tan. White patches are highly undesirable. Weight varies considerably, but should preferably be between 3 and 10 pounds. The breed standard does not specify height.

Bulldog *Britain*

The Bulldog is essentially a British breed; indeed, in a popular nineteenth century song Britishers were described as 'boys of the Bulldog breed'

Top: Bulldog.
Above: Bullmastiff.
Top right: Cairn Terrier.
Right: Bull Terrier.

due to their pugnacity.

In the fourteenth century, Bulldogs were used in bullbaiting; the dogs were trained to seize the bull by the nose and not let go until the bull fell. Since then, thanks to a few dedicated breeders, the temperament has much improved.

The Bulldog is thick set and broad, slightly higher at the loins than at the shoulders. The head is large with a short muzzle and a turned-up lower jaw protruding considerably in front of the upper jaw. It has dark eyes and small 'rose ears.' The tail is short, the coat close and smooth.

Color varies considerably, mostly in combination with white, and most varieties are acceptable. Weight is usually around 55 pounds: the breed standard does not specify height.

Bullmastiff *Britain*

Outside Britain the heavy and powerful Bullmastiff is comparatively rare. The breed is believed to have resulted from crossbreeding Bulldogs with Mastiffs. In the nineteenth century poaching was rife and gamekeepers needed agile, aggressive dogs capable of attacking intruders and holding until ordered to release — but never savaging or mauling. This specification was met when the ferocious and determined Bulldog was crossed with the formidable but less aggressive Mastiff.

The Bullmastiff is massive and heavily built without appearing clumsy. The head is large and square with a short muzzle and dark eyes. The coat is short and close.

The color is brindle, fawn, or red with a dark mask round the eyes and on the muzzle. The height at the shoulder for dogs is 25 to 27 inches, 24 to 26 inches for bitches. The weight is 90 to 130 pounds.

Bull Terrier *Britain*

When bullbaiting became illegal in Britain, the British turned to dogfighting, and for this a type of dog was needed which was lithe and quick but just as strong and vicious as before. So Bulldogs were crossed with terriers and the result was a 'bull and terrier dog.' Other crosses were then made which gave the Bull Terrier its characteristic conformation and its more controllable temper.

It is strong and muscular without appearing clumsy. The head is a main feature; it is distinctly egg shaped. The coat is short and glossy. The color is white, brindle, or colored with white markings. There are neither weight nor height limits laid down in the breed standard, but the height at the shoulder is usually about 16 inches.

The Miniature Bull Terrier is what its name implies — a small-size Bull Terrier, with a height of not more than 14 inches and weighing not more than 20 pounds. As a breed it is recognized in comparatively few countries outside Britain.

Cairn Terrier *Britain*

The lively little Cairn Terrier is a very popular pet and companion. It comes from Inverness in Scotland, and in its early days the breed had much in common with the Skye Terrier.

The Cairn Terrier is an active and hardy little dog with a shaggy coat, a bold bearing, and a somewhat fox-like expression.

The color varies from sandy to nearly black. Darker shadings on ears and muzzle are very typical. The height at the shoulder is about 10 inches, the weight about 14 pounds.

Cavalier King Charles Spaniel *Britain*
The friendly, affectionate little Cavalier King
Charles Spaniel is often confused with its close
relative and forerunner, the English Toy Spaniel.

In conformation, the Cavalier resembles an
old hunting spaniel in miniature; it is active,
graceful, spirited, and sturdily built.

There are four color varieties: *black and tan*
(pure black with small brown markings), *Blenheim* (white with chestnut-red markings and a
white blaze on the forehead), *tricolor* (black and
white with small tan markings), and *ruby* (a
whole-colored rich red). The breed standard does
not specify height at the shoulder. The weight is
10 to 18 pounds.

Chesapeake Bay Retriever *USA*
The Chesapeake Bay Retriever is the American
'water dog.' It is strikingly similar in build to the
British Labrador Retriever, but the Chesapeake
Bay Retriever has pure yellow eyes and a very
special coat: slightly wavy on the back and very
short, tough, and thick on the body in order to
withstand icy waters. The coat should feel decidedly oily to the touch and should be so water-
resistant that once the dog has come ashore and
given itself a shake, it should feel hardly damp!
The color is also considered very important; in
order that the dog should merge with its background as far as possible, the breed standard lays
down a 'dead grass' color ranging from dark
brown to faded tan. Dogs stand 23 to 26 inches
at the shoulder, bitches 21 to 24 inches.

Chihuahua *Mexico*

There are two breeds of the world's smallest dog, which is named after the Mexican state and city of Chihuahua: the Long-coat Chihuahua and the Smooth-coat Chihuahua. The Long-coat is identical to the Smooth-coat except for its long and soft-textured coat, which is either flat or slightly wavy and particularly abundant on ears, neck, and tail.

The Chihuahua is a neat, alert little dog with a saucy expression. The skull is 'apple domed,' the eyes round and dark or matching the color of the coat. Ruby eyes are considered very desirable.

Any color or mixture of colors is acceptable. The weight should be up to 6 pounds, preferably 2 to 4 pounds. The breed standard does not specify height.

Left: Chesapeake Bay Retriever.
Right: Smooth-coat Chihuahua.
Below: Chow Chow blue.

Chow Chow *China*

The Chow Chow came originally from China where, up to about 1000 BC, it was used as a temple dog to frighten off evil spirits. For this purpose Chows with a frowning and threatening expression were preferred. The breed came to Europe in the eighteenth century and has since become very popular as a companion and pet.

The Chow has a dignified bearing and aloof expression. It is active and well balanced but with a stilted gait. The head is large and broad with small, slightly rounded erect ears and has a bluish-black tongue. The body is short and level, the legs well boned and straight. The tail, set high, is carried well over the back.

There is a smooth-coated variety, but this is very rare. Normally the Chow has a thick, straight coat, particularly abundant round the neck. The color is black, red, fawn, cream, blue, or white, never particolored. The height at the shoulder is at least 18 inches.

Clumber Spaniel *Britain*

The Clumber Spaniel is rare enough in its home country and it is even more of a rarity outside Britain. The Clumber breed had its heyday toward the end of the nineteenth century when it was used as a sporting dog. The Clumber is a heavy and massive dog with a thoughtful expression. As a gundog breed it also needs to be active. The head is large and square with a broad skull and pronounced occiput (lower back part of the skull). The muzzle is heavy and deep with a flesh-colored nose, the eyes are dark and the ears large and vine-leaf shaped. The body is long and heavy and the legs short, very well boned, and strong. The tail is short, the coat close, silky, and straight. The legs, tail, and belly (but not the ears) are well feathered.

The color is white with smaller lemon markings. Weight varies from 45 to 70 pounds.

Cocker Spaniel *USA*

The Cocker Spaniel is an interesting example of what can happen when a breed moves from one country to another. The British introduced spaniels to America, which gradually, and without any mixture of strange blood, managed to become so different and 'American' in type that they were eventually recognized as a separate breed. This more extreme and showy spaniel variety has been popular as a pet for a long time in America.

The Cocker Spaniel is usually slightly smaller than the English variety. Its coat, which is either straight or wavy, is much more profuse than that of the ordinary Cocker, especially on the ears, legs, and belly. The color varies from black, black and tan, to particolors or roans.

Collie *Britain*

There are two varieties of Collie, the Rough Collie and the Smooth Collie. The Rough Collie is the popular sheepdog of the Scottish Highlands. Originally it was an insignificant farm dog, one among many, but as the best ones were picked as sheepdogs the type gradually stabilized.

The Rough Collie is elegant and active, but also strongly built. The color is usually sable and white, tricolor or blue merle (a marbled blue with white). The height at the shoulder is 22 to 24 inches for dogs, 20 to 22 inches for bitches. The weight is 40 to 65 pounds.

The Smooth Collie is comparatively rare both in Britain and outside its home country. With the exception of the coat, it conforms to the standard of the Rough Collie.

Curly-coated Retriever *Britain*

The coat of the Curly-coated Retriever distinguishes it from other retriever breeds and indicates its Irish Water Spaniel and Poodle ancestry. In addition to this lineage it is also descended from the same type of Old English hunting spaniel and Canadian dogs as the Golden and Labrador Retrievers. As an established breed it is, however, one of the oldest within the group.

The Curly-coated Retriever is a strong, smart dog with great stamina. The head is powerful with a moderately flat skull, the eyes are black or brown and rather large, but not too prominent. The ears are small, lying close to the head. The neck, body, and legs are strong and muscular. The tail is moderately short and is carried fairly straight. The coat is the main characteristic of the breed: it is a mass of small, crisp curls all over, including the ears and tail but excluding the muzzle. The close-fitting coat is impervious to water. The color is black or liver.

Dachshund *Germany*

The Dachshund (which means in German 'Badger dog') is one of the most popular breeds and it has evolved into six varieties; there are now standard and miniature sizes in Long-haired, Smooth-haired, and Wire-haired Dachshunds.

Short-legged terriers, which were the ancestors of the modern Dachshund, existed in Germany over a thousand years ago. In the early days the Dachshund was used for hunting underground, and more recently for tracking game and delivering it to the guns. Now Dachshunds are kept mainly as pets.

There are two smaller versions of the Dachshund: the Miniature Dachshund and an even smaller type known in some countries as the 'Rabbit' Dachshund. These miniatures evolved in Germany at the turn of this century, mainly through crosses between the smallest of the standard varieties. The Miniatures and 'Rabbit' Dachshunds can be either wire-haired, smooth-haired, or long-haired.

The Dachshund is active, bold, and alert. It is short-legged with a long body and proud carriage. The head is long and well chiselled and tapers gradually to the nose. The eyes are almond-shaped and should not be lighter than chestnut brown. The ears are rounded and lie close to the cheek. The neck is long and moderately arched, the back long and slightly curved over the loin, the legs short, straight, and well boned.

The color varies from black and tan to red, chocolate, brindle, and dapple. A standard Dachshund of average size should weigh not more than 20 pounds.

Dalmatian *Yugoslavia*

The name Dalmatian implies that this breed hails from Dalmatia on the Adriatic coast, and Yugoslavia is taken to be its official native country. But there is no real proof to indicate that this is so, and because there is some evidence of Dalmatians accompanying gypsies from the Far East during the Middle Ages, India is now favored as the most likely country of origin.

The Dalmatian is an agile, symmetrical, and muscular dog with active movement. Eye color depends on the markings and may even be yellow in liver-spotted dogs.

Color and markings are its most prominent characteristics. The ideal Dalmatian is evenly marked all over with small, round, black or liver spots. The height at the shoulder is 20 inches.

Inset top left: Blue merle Rough Collie.
Inset center left: Smooth-haired Dachshund.
Inset below left: wire haired Dachshund.
Left: Curly-coated Retriever.
Below: Dalmatian.

Inset left: Dandie Dinmont.
Left: Dobermann Pinscher.
Below: Cocker Spaniel.
Bottom: English Setter.

Dandie Dinmont *Britain*

The Dandie Dinmont Terrier is an unusual breed and in many parts of the world it is regarded as a canine curiosity. Originally the Dandie Dinmont was a wire-haired hunting terrier but, after its sudden climb to popularity in the nineteenth century, it was bred to fit more easily into drawing-room life and developed its present quaint looks.

It is a long-bodied, short-legged dog with a large head profusely covered with soft silky hair. The body is low at the shoulders with an arch over the loins and a slight drop from the loin toward the root of the tail. The tail is moderately long and carried in line with the back or slightly above it; the coat is a mixture of soft and fairly hard hair.

The color ranges from a dark bluish-black to a pale fawn. The height at the shoulder is 8 to 11 inches and the ideal weight is about 18 pounds.

Dobermann Pinscher *Germany*

The Dobermann Pinscher is named after the German dog catcher Dobermann, who at the turn of the twentieth century used some of his stray dogs to breed as mean and as vicious a dog as possible. Conformation was of secondary importance, but as far as temperament was concerned he succeeded beyond expectation. After Dobermann's time, the breed was crossed with, among others, Manchester Terriers and Greyhounds and has since improved in conformation and become more manageable in temperament.

Today's Dobermann is a clean-cut, powerful, and elegant dog. Indeed it is said that a first-class Dobermann is one of the most handsome creatures of the canine world. Its color is black or liver brown with tan markings. Dogs stand about 26 inches at the shoulder, bitches about 25 inches. The weight is about 55 pounds.

English Cocker Spaniel *Britain*

The English Cocker Spaniel is one of the most popular breeds in the world. It deserves to be so, for it is a friendly little dog with a cheerful temperament. It is, in fact, a sporting dog and, although it is more often kept as a pet, it usually manages to find some suitable outlet for its boundless energy. Although the spaniel type has been known for centuries in Britain, the Cocker was not recognized by the American Kennel Club as a breed until 1941.

The head is cleanly chiselled with flat cheeks and a marked stop. The eyes are full and of a color harmonizing with the coat. The ears are low-set, long, and supple. The body is compact and deep, the legs well boned with round feet. The tail is docked fairly short, is carried low, and is incessantly active. The coat is smooth and silky with long, soft feathering on the ears, chest, and on the back of the legs.

The color may vary from solid colors to particolors or roans (white speckled with black, lemon, orange, or liver). The ideal height at the shoulder is about 16 inches.

English Foxhound *Britain*

The English Foxhound is a thoroughbred, and one of the best known, most publicized, frequently painted and photographed of any English dog.

Looks are of secondary importance to working abilities and breed type varies a great deal. The color is usually tan with a black saddle, and white markings on the foreface, chest, belly, legs, and tail, or white with black, tan, or lemon markings. The height at the shoulder is about 24 inches.

The main difference between the American Foxhound and its English ancestor breed is size. The American dog is generally a bigger, long-legged dog with a strong body. Otherwise there is little to distinguish the two breeds.

English Setter *Britain*

Most people would concede that the English Setter, with his graceful lines, limpid eyes, and the friendly nature symbolized by his gently waving tail, is one of the most attractive of all breeds of dog.

The English Setter has an appearance of elegance, strength, and speed. The head is long with a marked stop, straight, deep muzzle, and expressive, dark eyes. The back slopes toward the scimitar-shaped tail which tapers off toward the tip. The long and glossy coat is particularly long on the ears, chest, tail, and on the back of the legs.

In color, white predominates with markings in black, lemon, or liver; sometimes tricolor (black, white, and tan). The height at the shoulder is about 25 inches.

English Springer Spaniel *Britain*
The English Springer is the most robust variety of spaniel, and it is credited with an even temperament.

The English Springer Spaniel is a medium-sized, strong, and active dog. The color of the eyes and the nose harmonizes with the coat color. The ears are large but not as long as the Cocker's and are set higher. The tail is low set, often with a lively action. The coat is short and glossy on the body and head, and thick, fairly long, and slightly wavy on the ears, chest, under the body, and on the back of the legs.

The color is usually white with black or liver markings. The height at the shoulder for dogs is about 20 inches, bitches are slightly smaller.

English Toy Spaniel *Britain*
The English Toy Spaniel was at one time more popular and more common than its close relative, the Cavalier King Charles Spaniel. Nowadays the position is reversed. The basic difference between the two breeds is that the former has a flatter nose than the Cavalier and is frequently smaller.

There are four color varieties: King Charles (black and tan), Blenheim (white and chestnut), Prince Charles (tricolor: white, black, and tan), and Ruby (whole-colored rich red). The breed standard does not specify height. The desirable weight is 6 to 12 pounds.

Field Spaniel *Britain*
The Field Spaniel shares the ancestry of the other spaniel breeds, but has remained a working breed and is normally seen at field trials rather than at formal dog shows.

It is a well-balanced sporting dog with a docile temperament. The head is similar to that of the Cocker, but is not as distinctive and is really more like a setter's. The body and bone are lighter than the Cocker's and the coat is less profuse, forming silky feathering similar to an Irish Setter.

As in most other spaniel breeds, there are several color varieties, but black, black and tan, roan, or solid-color shades of liver are preferable to particolors. The height at the shoulder is about 18 inches.

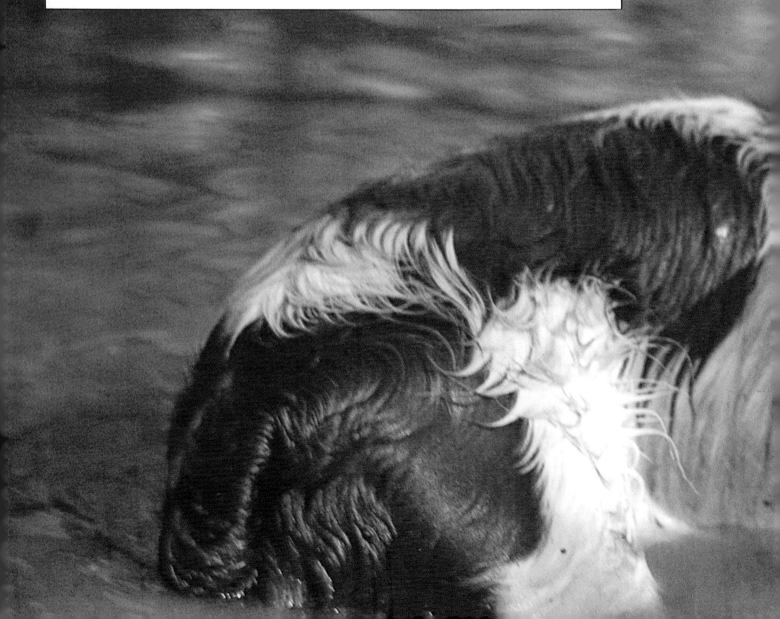

Flat-coated Retriever *Britain*

This is a fairly uncommon sporting dog breed — distinguished, of course, by its flat coat. Its ancestors are believed to have been Newfoundland dogs which accompanied Canadian seafarers to British ports; later these dogs were interbred with setters and pointers. But it is the Labrador Retriever which is thought to have been responsible for the evolution of the flat coat.

The Flat-coated Retriever is a powerful animal, yet it does not give the appearance of being either cumbersome or lanky. The eyes are hazel or dark brown and the ears are small and carried close to the side of the head. The coat is close, fine in texture, and should be as flat as possible. Fore- and hindquarters are well feathered.

The color is black or liver. The height at the shoulder is about 23 inches and the weight between 60 and 70 pounds.

Inset left: Flat-coated Retriever.
Left: English Springer Spaniel.
Inset below: Field Spaniel.

Fox Terrier *Britain*

Basically there are two categories of Fox Terrier — the wire-haired breed and the Smooth Fox Terrier. In effect the Wire-haired Fox Terrier is generally regarded as *the* terrier. This is because of its temperament and attitude, for it embodies all the typical terrier-like characteristics — keenness and alertness coupled with a slight aggressiveness. These features have made it one of the most popular breeds in the world. The Wire-haired Fox Terrier is square built and energetic. Its coat is wiry with abundant whiskers and leg hair. White predominates, but otherwise color is of little importance. Dogs stand just over 15 inches at the shoulder with a weight of about 18 pounds; bitches are proportionately smaller and lighter.

The Smooth Fox Terrier is believed to have evolved from crosses between its wire-haired relative and other dogs used for hunting foxes. In appearance — apart from the coat — very little separates the two varieties, but the head tapers slightly more from the ears toward the eyes and the muzzle is slightly more pointed. The coat should be smooth, thick, and close; the belly and underside of the thighs should be covered. Color, height, and weight are the same as for the Wire-haired Fox Terrier.

Finally, the essentials of the Fox Terrier have been defined as: weight 18 pounds, color is usually white with black and tan markings, ears are carried erect; the muzzle is narrow but relatively long; and the tail should be docked fairly short.

French Bulldog *France*

The French Bulldog is descended from Bulldogs exported to France from Britain and interbred with various Continental toy breeds.

The French Bulldog is compactly built, well boned, and thick set. Despite its slightly pugnacious expression, it is a friendly dog. The body is higher at the loins than at the shoulder, but the front legs should not be crooked. The coat is smooth and lustrous.

The color is brindle, white, pied, or fawn. The American Kennel Club has two classes: lightweights under 22 pounds, and heavyweights over 22 pounds but under a maximum of 28 pounds.

German Shepherd *Germany*

The Deutsche Schäferhund is probably the most internationally popular breed. And over the years it has had more publicity, good and bad, than all the other breeds of dogs put together. The German Shepherd's highly developed senses make it ideally suited to training in a variety of fields — with the police, the armed forces, and the blind.

The German Shepherd did not become a breed in the real sense until the latter half of the nineteenth century, and the way it looks today is the

Top: Smooth-haired Fox Terrier.
Above: German Shepherd.
Right: French Bulldog.

result of only a few decades of intensive and skillful German breeding. Predominantly native breeds form the foundation of the German Shepherd, from pure spitz breed types to dogs on sheepdog lines.

The German Shepherd is active, alert, and good natured. The color is usually shades of gray to black with even, lighter markings. White or near white is not considered desirable. The height at the shoulder for dogs is 24 to 26 inches, for bitches 22 to 24 inches.

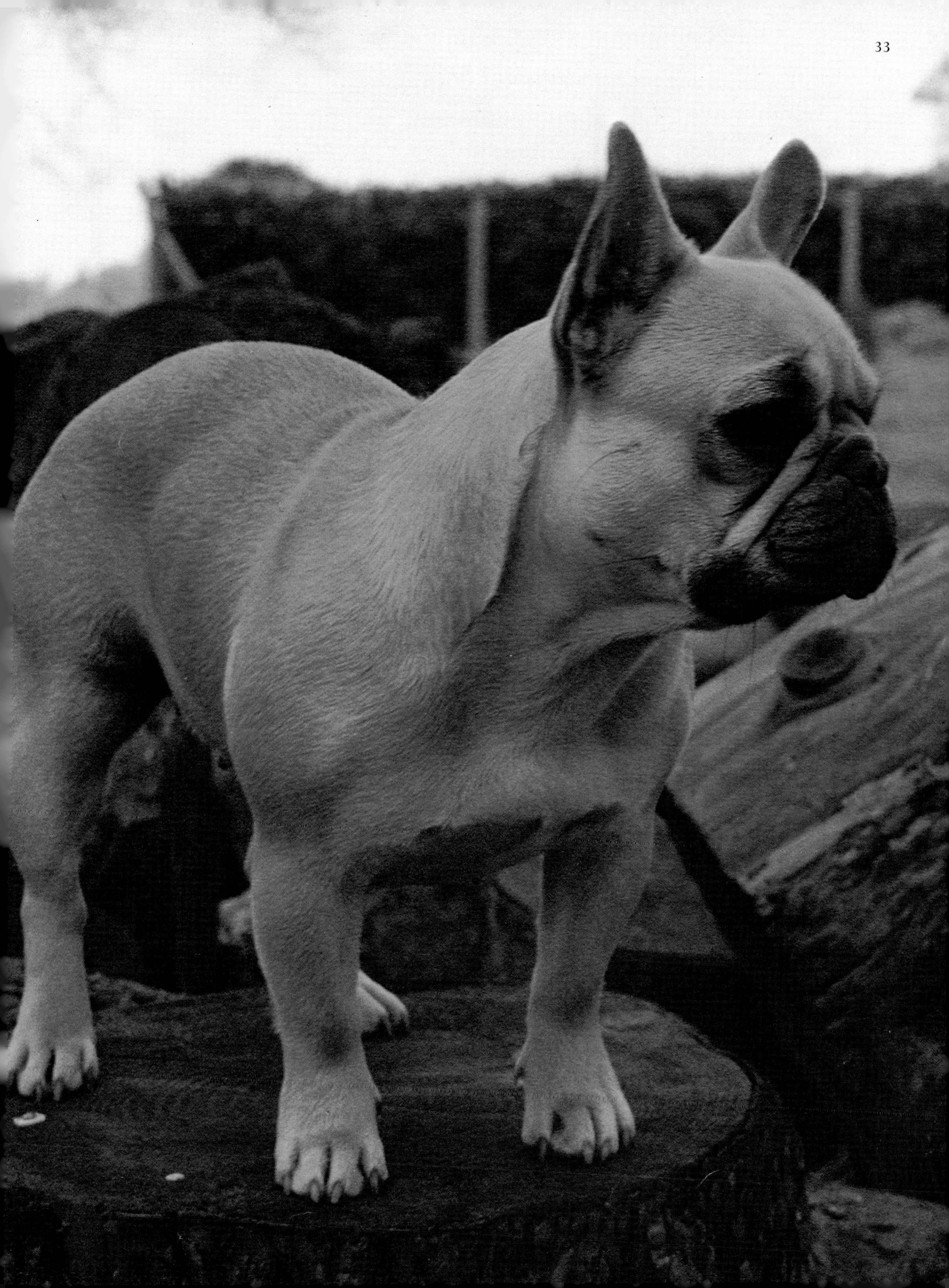

German Short-haired Pointer *Germany*
The Deutscher Vorstehhund, Kurzhaar, is one of the best-known sporting dogs in the world. Sportsmen appreciate the dog that has evolved not only for its ability to find, 'point-up,' flush, and retrieve game, but also because of the German pointer's willingness to face sleet, heavy cover, and to go into cold, rough water to retrieve a duck.

A German Short-haired Pointer is classy without being too elegant and powerful without being too heavy. The ears are soft and hang close to the head; the nose is solid brown. The back is slightly sloping, the chest well developed, and the legs muscular with well-bent stifles. The tail is docked to medium length, about two-thirds from the root. The coat is thick and short but fairly coarse. Except for a longer coat, the Long-haired Pointer is identical.

The color is liver, liver and white spotted, or liver and white ticked. Dogs stand 23 to 25 inches at the shoulder, bitches 21 to 23 inches. Dogs weigh 55 to 70 pounds.

German Wire-haired Pointer *Germany*

The German Wire-haired Pointer breed was developed by crossing the offspring of a number of other breeds – the Wire-haired Pointing Griffon, the Stichelhaar (a retriever), the Pudel-pointer (Poodle Pointer), the German Short-haired Pointer, and possibly the English Pointer. The result was that it was some time before a true breed emerged and, until it did, the various types competed against each other to find favor with sportsmen.

Except for the coat, the German Wire-haired conforms to the standard of the short-haired variety. The coat is rough and close all over except on the ears, eyebrows, and jaws where it is more profuse, giving it bushy eyebrows, beard, and whiskers. The height for dogs is 24 to 26 inches, and bitches not less than 22 inches.

Inset: German Long-haired Pointer.
Below: German Short-haired Pointer.

Golden Retriever *Britain*

The Golden Retriever is a delightful and adaptable animal equally capable of becoming a first-class sporting dog, a good-natured companion, or a conscientious guide dog for the blind. Since the end of World War II it has become increasingly popular as a pet because of its friendly temperament.

The origin of the breed dates back to the second half of the nineteenth century when a yellow dog bred from Flat-coated Retriever parents was mated to a little liver-colored English Retriever. The direct progeny of this union proved to be excellent sporting dogs, the strain was largely kept pure, and by the beginning of this century the Golden Retriever began to establish itself.

The Golden Retriever is a well-proportioned dog; active, docile, powerful, and yet stylish. The coat is either flat or wavy, close, water-resistant, and with good feathering, especially on the tail.

The color may be any shade of gold or cream, neither too dark nor too light. Dogs stand 22 to 24 inches at the shoulder, bitches 20 to 22 inches, while weight is about 67 and 57 pounds respectively.

Gordon Setter *Britain*

The Gordon Setter is slightly larger than the English Setter and does not have quite the same elegant appearance. The ears are soft and lie close to the head. The tail is fairly short and straight, and in action is carried horizontally or below the line of the back. The coat is short and fine, but forms long and silky featherings on the ears, belly, tail, and back of legs.

The color is always black with smaller chestnut-red markings on the muzzle, chest, and underside of the body. A white spot on the chest is allowed, but not desirable. The height at the shoulder is about 26 inches for dogs and about 24 inches for bitches. The weight (dogs) is about 55 to 80 pounds.

Left: Gordon Setter.
Right: Great Dane.

Great Dane *Germany*

The breed known as the Great Dane *may* have originated in Denmark — hence the name linking it with that country. There is no doubt that it was in Germany that the breed reached its present standard of excellence. Its ancestors were the heavy Mastiff-type war dogs attached to Caesar's Roman legions. Their progeny were used by continental noblemen for hunting.

The ideal Great Dane is a combination of strength and elegance. Viewed from the side, the head, which is carried proudly, is broad and deep with a pronounced stop and a deep muzzle. The ears may be carried close to the head or cropped. The coat is short and sleek. The minimum height of an adult dog should be 30 inches, that of a bitch 28 inches. The minimum weight for dogs is 120 pounds, bitches 100 pounds.

Greyhound *Britain*

Greyhounds have been used for coursing game for centuries – certainly from Roman times, if not earlier. Moreover, it appears that over the centuries they have retained a greater purity of form than most other breeds.

The name 'greyhound' probably derives from the fact that gray was at one time the most usual color for dogs of this breed, but it is also possible that it may come from 'gaze' – a word which was descriptive of a dog which hunts by sight. The latter would be more appropriate because the Greyhound was employed until modern times for coursing deer, stag, gazelle, fox, and hare. Since World War I the Greyhound has generally been restricted to an artificial form of coursing – on the racetrack. Greyhound racing continues to be immensely popular but in recent years the Greyhound has come to be appreciated as a pet – a role for which, because of its gentle and affectionate nature, it is ideally suited.

The Greyhound is a classy, muscular, and supple dog. All colors are acceptable in any shade from black to white, self-colored or particolored. The height at the shoulder is between 28 and 30 inches for dogs, and between 27 and 28 inches for bitches. The weight for dogs is 65 to 70 pounds, bitches 60 to 65 pounds.

Ibizan Hound *Spain*

The Ibizan Hound takes its name from the Balearic island of Ibiza, where it is said to have originated – although it is claimed that the best examples of the breed are found on the neighboring island of Majorca, where they are used to hunt hares and partridges.

Three types of Ibizan Hound exist: smooth-haired, wire-haired, and long-haired. They are strongly built, very agile, very astute, intelligent, and docile, and they can jump to a great height without a take-off run.

The Ibizan Hound is white with red or fawn patches, or self-colored in any of these colors. The eyes are amber and the nose liver-colored. The height at the shoulder for dogs is 24 to 26 inches, 22 to 25 inches for bitches.

Irish Setter *Britain*

The rich chestnut color of the Irish Setter's coat is such a jealously preserved characteristic that the Irish formed a breed club over a century ago to protect the pure red color from any intermingling of blood from particolored dogs.

Unfortunately, the latter type proved to be more useful as gundogs, and the preference of the Irish for a pure red dog meant that their setter became less widely used than the particolored dogs. But the Irish Setter has retained its great attraction, becoming one of the most fashionable show dogs.

With its striking color and its dark, expressive eyes combined with a lively and friendly temperament, the Irish Setter is possibly the most attractive of all the pointing gundog breeds. The coat is sleek, longer on the ears, chest, tail, and back of legs.

The color is always a glossy, rich chestnut with no trace of other shades. The height at the shoulder is usually about 24 inches and the weight is around 55 pounds.

Below left: A Greyhound puppy.
Below: Irish Setter.
Right: Ibizan Hound.
Inset right: Irish Terrier.

Irish Terrier *Britain*

The Irish Terrier is a comparatively recent breed. They are inquisitive and venturesome, and they make ideal companions. In size the Irish Terriers are midway between the Welsh or Lakeland terriers and the Airedale. Yet, in spite of their terrier qualities and convenient size, they have never quite caught on either as a pet or as a show dog.

The Irish Terrier is active, lively, and behaves with cocky self-assurance. The head is long and fairly narrow; the eyes are dark and fiery. The tail is docked slightly longer than in most other terriers and is carried erect, not over the back. The coat is wiry, close, and not so long as to hide the outline of the body.

The Irish Terrier is whole-colored, the most desirable color being shades of red. The height at the shoulder is about 18 inches, with the weight around 26 pounds.

Irish Water Spaniel *Britain*

The more one looks at an Irish Water Spaniel, the harder it is to believe that it is a true spaniel. Not only is it much larger than the other varieties, it is also completely different in shape and general characteristics. In many ways it resembles the Poodle, a breed which must figure among its ancestors.

In fact the Irish Water Spaniel has evolved from several different types of spaniel common in Ireland and Scotland toward the end of the nineteenth century.

It is a sturdily built dog, eager and intelligent. The eyes are small, brown, and alert; the ears very long, low-set, and covered with twisted curls. The coat is an important characteristic: it has a natural oiliness and is composed of dense, tight ringlets — profuse everywhere except on the muzzle, just above the eyes, and on the tail where the ringlets stop abruptly a few inches below the root.

The color is always a dark liver with a purplish tint. The height at the shoulder for dogs is about 21 to 23 inches, 20 to 22 inches for bitches.

Irish Wolfhound *Eire*

The Irish Wolfhound is one of the tallest dogs in the world, and the breed is also one of the oldest. For centuries Irish Wolfhounds were used by the Irish Celts for hunting, and they were famous throughout the Western world.

With its great size, impressive bulk, and rough gray coat, it would seem that the Wolfhound has everything needed to make it the ideal, awe-inspiring guard. Its threatening presence, however, is softened by its gentle, dark eyes and an affectionate, friendly disposition. As a pet the Wolfhound is docile and manageable and, partly because of these attributes, needs less space than one would imagine.

The Irish Wolfhound is muscular and strongly, though gracefully, built. The coat is rough and especially long on the head. The color is usually a shade of gray, but may be black, white, fawn, red, or brindle. The minimum height for dogs is 32 inches, weight 120 pounds; bitches 30 inches and 105 pounds.

Italian Greyhound *Italy*

The Italian Greyhound is the smallest of the sight-hound breeds, but it belongs to the great Greyhound family. Italian Greyhounds were originally bred from the smallest greyhounds, resulting in a miniature breed. For centuries this graceful and elegant miniature Greyhound has been a popular pet, and today Italian Greyhounds are raced in some countries. They are very gentle and affectionate by nature and make excellent house dogs.

In the show ring, great emphasis is placed on its elegance, fine bone, and high-stepping, graceful action. It is well proportioned and sound, without appearing dwarfish, and is not as

Left: Irish Water Spaniel.
Right: Keeshond.
Inset right: Japanese Chin.

delicate as it may appear. In many respects it resembles its larger cousins, the Whippet and the Greyhound, but it is not only smaller but more slender in all respects.

Desirable color and markings vary slightly from country to country; fawn, cream, or blue, however, are always acceptable. The size and weight, too, vary between countries. Generally a weight not exceeding 10 pounds and a height at the shoulder of between 13 and 15 inches are considered the most desirable.

Japanese Chin *Japan*

The Japanese Chin and the Pekingese have a great deal in common and it is thought that they share a common oriental ancestry. The Japanese Chin has, however, longer legs than the Pekingese, a lighter body, and moves more gracefully.

They make delightful and handsome pets. The head is fairly large and rounded with a flat nose and a slight 'wrinkle' on the upper lip. The eyes are large and dark with the whites clearly showing at the inner corners. The coat is profuse and long, free from curl, and particularly abundant on the tail, thighs, front legs, and feet.

The color is always white with evenly distributed patches in black or a shade of red. Size varies and, though the smaller the better, it may have a height at shoulder of up to 11 inches.

Keeshond *Holland*

The Keeshond (pronounced 'kayshond') is named after a celebrated eighteenth-century Dutch patriot, who owned one of the spitz-type dogs which were the predecessors of the modern Keeshond. For centuries these dogs were used as guard dogs and as barge dogs on the Dutch canals.

Keeshonds thrive on companionship and are dependable pets. The Keeshond is short and compact with a bold expression. A unique feature of the breed is the so-called 'spectacles,' that is, lighter shadings round the dark, almond-shaped eyes. The ears are small and erect, the body deep and sturdy, and the tail tightly curled, even with a double curl, over the back. The coat is thick and straight, hanging loosely from the body, and is particularly abundant around the neck, where it forms a large ruff, and on the buttocks.

The color is all gray with dark tips. The height at the shoulder is about 18 inches for dogs, 17 inches for bitches.

Kerry Blue Terrier *Eire*

The Kerry Blue Terrier has its background deep in the remoteness of southwest Ireland. It has been said that Kerry Blues have Irish Wolfhound blood in them, and it has also been suggested that the color and coat texture were enhanced by the introduction of Bedlington Terriers. Whatever the background, it has since 1920 become popular in both Britain and the United States.

In size the Kerry Blue stands midway between the Airedale and the Bedlington. Puppies and young dogs are always black and all too frequently the desired blue color never appears, even in fully grown animals. The height at the shoulder for dogs is 18 to 19 inches, slightly less for bitches. The ideal weight is about 35 pounds.

Komondor *Hungary*

The Komondor is the largest of the Hungarian dogs used for guarding flocks of sheep and herds of cattle. It is of Asian origin and is probably related to Russian herding dogs. The Komondor has a long and profuse coat (which by tradition in Hungary is never groomed). This coat, which consists of either flat or round 'cords,' protects it as effectively from the heat in summer as from the cold in winter. The Komondor has also proved to be an excellent pet and has become quite popular as a show dog. They make very good watchdogs.

The color is always white. The height for dogs ranges from 26 to 32 inches.

Kuvasz *Hungary*

The Kuvasz is an old breed whose ancestors are believed to have been taken to Hungary by the Kurds about AD 1100. Its name is a corruption of the Turkish word *kawasz*, which means 'guardian of the peace.' Originally a sheepdog, the breed was also used to hunt wild boar. Nowadays they have reverted to their original guard-dog role, but their watchfulness, size, and great strength plus friendly temperament have also made them popular as household companions.

A typical Kuvasz is tall and powerful, and moves in a slow, dignified manner. The shape of the head is very important; it is noble and expressive and the foreface is neither sharp nor coarse. The eyes are dark brown with a fierce expression. The tail is carried low except when the dog is alert, in which case it may be slightly raised; the tip of the tail is often hooked. The coat is short on the head, ears, and feet but long, wavy, and fairly coarse, especially around the neck, on the tail, and on the back of the legs.

The color is pure white, but ivory shades are acceptable. The height at the shoulder is 28 to 30 inches for dogs, and 26 to 27 inches for bitches.

Labrador Retriever *Britain*

The aristocratic but powerfully built Labrador Retriever is a true British breed, despite its name. Some of its ancestors, however, were Newfoundland dogs taken to Britain by Canadian fishermen who sailed there to sell their catches. Subsequently the breed was developed by crossbreeding in order to produce sporting dogs, and has gained great popularity both as a working dog and as a pet.

The general appearance of the Labrador is that of a strongly built, powerful dog. Its color is usually black or yellow, though some are liver and these may be lighter in eye and have a liver-colored nose. The height at the shoulder is about 22 inches for dogs, 21 to 22 inches for bitches.

Above left: Kerry Blue Terrier.
Above: Labrador Retriever.
Right: Komondor.
Inset right: Lakeland Terrier.

Lakeland Terrier *Britain*

The Lakeland Terrier hails from the Lake District in Cumbria, the English Border country adjoining Scotland. It is in fact a comparatively recent breed, bred originally for work with Border farmers, plagued with foxes which preyed on the young sheep.

The Lakeland Terrier may easily be mistaken for the Welsh Terrier, although it is more heavily built, usually has more coat on the head and the legs, and has a greater variety of colors. The head is well balanced with powerful jaws. The eyes are larger than the Fox Terrier's and the back only moderately short. The tail, as with most terriers, is set and carried high; the coat is rough.

The color varies from whole-colored wheaten to pure black. The height at the shoulder should not exceed just over 14 inches. The weight is usually about 16 pounds.

Lhasa Apso *Tibet*

The Lhasa Apso is a Tibetan toy breed. It is fairly rare in some countries and is often mistaken for the more common Shih Tzu. In fact the Apso is a true Tibetan dog, while the Shih Tzu is said to have originated in western China. However the two breeds undoubtedly mixed.

The Lhasa or Tibetan Apso is 10 to 11 inches high at the shoulder. The weight is 8 to 15 pounds. The most common color is golden (other colors are sandy, honey, dark grizzle, slate, smoke, particolors, black, white or brown). The coat is heavy, straight, hard, and dense, of medium length and parted along the spine. The head is heavily covered with hair, with a fall over the eyes. The nose is black, the eyes dark, the ears pendant and heavily feathered.

Maltese *Italy*

The gay, good-natured little Maltese is the oldest toy breed in the West. It probably takes its name not from the island of Malta as one might expect, but from the Sicilian town of Melita.

Underneath its flowing coat, the Maltese has a rather low-set body. The luxuriant coat is the breed's most prominent feature: it is very long all over, straight and silky and nearly reaches the ground.

Pure white is the most desirable color, but all colors are acceptable – according to the Italian breed standard – as long as the dog is not parti-colored. In common with most toy breeds, the Maltese should be as small as possible. The weight should not exceed 8 pounds and the height at the shoulder should not be above 10 inches for both dogs and bitches.

Manchester Terrier *Britain*

This breed supposedly originated in Manchester as the result of mating what was described as an 'English' terrier with a Whippet. The aim was to produce a breed that would kill rats and catch rabbits.

In appearance the Manchester Terrier resembles the Smooth Fox Terrier, with which it has much in common. The head is long and narrow, the eyes are small, set close, dark, and sparkling. The neck is long and slightly arched, the back moderately curved and the tail, which is carried low, is thick at the root and tapers to a point. The coat is smooth, short, and glossy.

The background color must be black with rich mahogany tan markings on muzzle, cheeks, above eyes, below knees, on each side of the chest, and on the vent. The height at shoulder is about 16 inches for dogs, 15 inches for bitches. The weight should not be more than 22 pounds.

In recent years the Toy Manchester Terrier has become a popular variety. The standard for the Toy is the same, except that weight should not exceed 12 pounds, and ear specifications differ.

Mastiff/Old English Mastiff *Britain*

Before pure-bred dogs were recognized as such, any large dog was often called a Mastiff. Today, only three breeds are classified as Mastiffs, of which the best known is the Old English Mastiff. The other two are the rare Tibetan Mastiff and the Japanese Tosa.

The Old English Mastiff is a tall, powerful dog considerably bigger than its relative the Bull-mastiff, but not as heavily built. Its nose is not as blunt although it is still broad and square; the eyes are small and dark. The Old English Mastiff has a greater reach of neck than the Bullmastiff and is considerably higher in the leg. The tail is fairly long; the coat is short and close. The color is usually apricot or fawn, with black on the muzzle and ears and around the eyes. Dogs stand about 30 inches at the shoulder, bitches $27\frac{1}{2}$ inches.

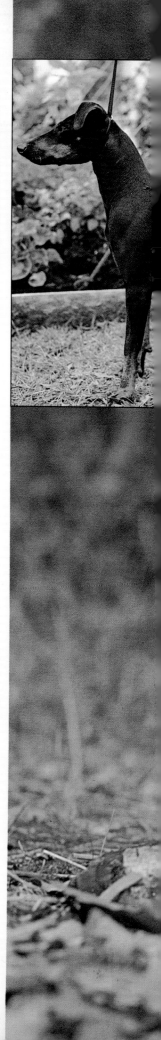

Miniature Pinscher *Germany*

Many people erroneously call the Miniature Pinscher a Miniature Dobermann. Although they do, in fact, bear a striking resemblance to each other, the Miniature Pinscher is a much older breed. It is a tiny, elegant, and lively little dog and one of the most popular toy breeds in the world. Characteristics are a narrow, wedge-shaped head, a square body with a deep chest, dark brown and piercing black eyes, and a black nose (except with chocolate-colored Pinschers, when it may be brown). The coat should be short and glossy.

The color should be red or lustrous black with tan markings. The ideal height at the shoulders should not exceed 12 inches and the weight is about 6 to 8 pounds.

Above left: Maltese.
Below left: Miniature Pinschers.
Above: Manchester Terrier.
Right: Old English Mastiff.

Newfoundland *Newfoundland*

There is much uncertainty about the origin of the massive Newfoundland dog. One American canine authority has claimed that it is descended from Pyrenean Mountain Dogs taken to Newfoundland in the middle of the seventeenth century by Basque fishermen. Other authorities believe that the Husky and other breeds may be counted among its ancestors. In any event the dog that evolved in the Newfoundland environment was particularly suited to the island.

His head is massive, has a distinct stop, and is free of wrinkles. The muzzle is square and deep; the eyes are small and brown and deep-set; ears, which are small and triangular with rounded tips, lie close to the head. The length of the dog's body from withers to base of tail is approximately equal to its height, though bitches may be slightly longer than tall. The large cat-like feet are completely webbed. The tail is broad, well furred, and reaches to below the hocks.

The Newfoundland has a water-resistant double coat, the outer coat being moderately long and full but straight and flat. The color is generally a dull black, but there may be a tinge of bronze or a splash of white on the toes or chest. Male Newfoundland dogs average 28 inches at the shoulder and weigh about 150 pounds. Bitches are slightly smaller.

Norfolk Terrier *Britain*

The Norfolk Terrier was recognized as a separate breed only comparatively recently. Until then it was regarded as a variety of Norwich Terrier. In effect the Norfolk differs from the Norwich in only a few minor points.

Norwegian Elkhound *Norway*

The Norwegian Elkhound – often known more simply as the Elkhound or Elk – is a working dog and a typical spitz breed. The sharp comparatively small but erect ears, the straight hocks, the ruff around the neck and the tail tightly curled over the back are all clear indicators of its origin. In effect its home and its task are given by its name. It was, and still is, used to hunt moose in Scandinavia in general and in Norway in particular. In temperament the Elk is bold and energetic – an effective guard dog, yet normally friendly but independent in character.

The Elkhound is of medium size and substance, with a compact short body, thick coat, and tail tightly curled over the center line of the back. The head is broad between the prick ears, muzzle broad at base, tapering gradually but not pointed. The stop is not large yet clearly defined. The eyes are very dark brown, medium in size, oval, not protruding. Ears are set high, firm and erect, pointed and with their height slightly greater than their width at base. The neck is of medium length, firm, and muscular. The body is square in profile with a wide straight back; the chest is broad and deep. The loins are muscular

and the feet compact with small, slightly oval, paws. The coat should be thick, hard, abundant, weather-resistant, and smooth lying. The color is generally a medium gray with black tips on the outer coat, a lighter shade on the chest, stomach, and underside of the tail. The weight is approximately 55 pounds for dogs and 48 pounds for bitches. The height at the shoulder is 18 to 20½ inches.

Norwich Terrier *Britain*

The Norwich Terrier is one of the smallest of the terriers, but it is said to be a 'demon' for its size. The breed was created by crossing the Irish Terrier with various short-legged terrier varieties and, like most British terriers, it takes its name from its place of origin.

The Norwich Terrier is a small, low, keen dog, compact and strong. It has a gay and fearless temperament and a lovable disposition. The head is not very long and has a well-defined stop; the skull is wide and slightly rounded. The eyes are dark, full of expression, bright, and keen; the ears can be erect or dropped. The tail is docked.

The color is red, red wheaten, black and tan, or grizzle. The height at the shoulder is about 10 inches.

Above: Norwegian Elkhound.
Right: Newfoundland.
Inset right: Norwich Terrier.

Old English Sheepdog *Britain*

Although it is called 'old,' the Old English Sheepdog is no more than 200 years old. Developed originally as a working dog to protect herds of cattle from beasts of prey, it has in recent years become a pet and companion.

The Old English Sheepdog is massively built, with an abundance of coat all over. It stands slightly higher at the loins than at the shoulder and this gives it a characteristic rolling gait. The coat is not only profuse but shaggy and of good, strong texture.

The color is usually gray, grizzle, or blue with or without white markings. The height at the shoulder for dogs is about 22 inches; bitches are slightly smaller.

Otter Hound *Britain*

The Otter Hound has been known in Britain since the fourteenth century. It has a remarkable scenting ability, and is used for otter hunting. It is a big, courageous dog thoroughly at home in water, but it has an ungainly body, a large head, and webbed feet. The ears are long, thin, and pendulous; the neck is moderately short and looks practically nonexistent because of the abundant ruff around it. The tail is carried upward but not curled and, like the rest of the dog, is covered with a crisp and oily coat, which should not be soft and woolly.

The color is usually a sandy fawn or grizzle with more or less diffuse black and tan markings. The shoulder height is about 24 to 26 inches; weight is about 65 pounds.

Papillon *France*

The Papillon derives its name from the fact that its ears, properly carried, should suggest an open-winged butterfly. It is a daintily balanced little toy dog with an attractive head, an alert bearing, and an intelligent and lively expression.

The Papillon was a great favorite of the aristocratic ladies of the French court prior to the French Revolution. Since 1793, more Papillons have been bred in Belgium and Britain than France, but it is claimed that the quality is equally high. The Papillon should be small and elegant, and the coat long and silky, forming profuse frills on the neck, chest, and thighs. The ears should be heavily fringed; the color white with black and/or red markings. The weight should be about 4 pounds and the height at the shoulder should not exceed 12 inches.

Pekingese *China*

The Pekingese has supposedly existed for 2000 years or more as the miniature dog of ancient China. It is certainly known that miniature dogs were kept as pets at the Imperial Court some 1500 years ago. In 1860, when the Summer Palace in Peking was sacked by British and French troops, five of the dogs were taken back to England. These dogs, mated with a few

more Pekingese obtained by less adventurous methods, subsequently formed the basis of the present modern breed. The Pekingese soon became universally popular.

The Pekingese is a small, well-balanced, bold, and dignified dog. He carries himself fearlessly with an alert and intelligent expression. His head is broad and he has large, lustrous eyes and a flat profile. The forequarters are thick-set and heavily boned with slightly bowed front legs, while the hindquarters are lighter and straight. The tail has a magnificent plume and is curved over the back. The coat is also particularly profuse on the neck, chest, thighs, and at the back of the front legs.

All colors except liver are acceptable. The height at the shoulder is 6 to 10 inches and the weight is 7 to 11 pounds for dogs, 8 to 12 pounds for bitches.

Above: Pekingese.
Inset right: Otter Hound.
Right: Old English Sheepdog.

Pharaoh Hound *Egypt*

The Pharaoh Hound belongs to the Greyhound family and bears a very strong resemblance to the hound with large, erect ears depicted in ancient Egyptian sculptures.

A medium-sized dog in build, it is very like the modern Ibizan Hound. It is noted for its clean-cut, graceful lines, its reach, and large, erect ears. The tail should be set fairly high and carried above the level of the back. The eyes are amber or dark brown and the coat short, glossy, and smooth.

The basic color is often white with patches of gray or red; predominantly red specimens are, however, most common. The height at the shoulder for dogs is 25 to 28 inches.

Pointer *Britain*

The name of this breed needs little or no explanation. The Pointer is a sporting dog which searches for game and, having found it, freezes and points with its nose. It is a beautiful and elegant animal, and is now as popular as a show dog as it is in the field.

The hallmarks of the Pointer are a clean outline and elegance in appearance and movement. The skull should be of medium breadth and in proportion to the length of the face; the stop should be well pronounced and the muzzle slightly concave. The eyes should be either hazel or brown according to the color of the coat. The ears, which are fairly large, should lie close to the head. The neck should be long and arched, with the back sloping away to well-angulated hindquarters. The tail should be thick at the root, growing gradually thinner to the point, and carried level with the back. The coat should be short, close, and shiny.

The color of the English Pointer is white with black, lemon, or liver markings, or black, liver, or lemon, with or without white. Dogs stand about 24 inches at the shoulder.

Pomeranian *Britain*

The Pomeranian is an attractive little dog, which evolved from German spitz breeds imported into Britain about a hundred years ago.

Today's ideal Pomeranian should be a compact, short-coupled dog — exhibiting great intelligence in his expression and activity and buoyancy in his deportment. It should have two coats, a soft, fluffy undercoat and a long, straight overcoat; the hair at the neck should be especially profuse so that it forms a frill which extends over the shoulders. The hindquarters and legs should be covered with long hair or feathering from the top of the rump to the hocks. The characteristic tail is set high and carried flat over the back, with the tip curled. Self-colored dogs are preferred. Orange is most common, but all colors are acceptable, even particolors. The weight is about 4 to 5 pounds, and the height at the shoulder should not exceed 11 inches.

Poodle *France*

Poodles come in three varieties: Standard, Miniature, and Toy Poodles. The Standard Poodle came first, and was originally used as a sporting dog. The outstanding features of the Poodle are its intelligence and its determination to please.

How long the breed has been established or where is not known. However, it is generally accepted that the Poodle is truly French, and that it is distantly related to the Foxhound and spaniel breeds.

A typical Poodle is a very active, intelligent, and elegant-looking dog, well built, with a proud carriage. His head is carried high, and he has a fairly narrow skull and a long foreface with well-defined chin. The eyes are almond-shaped, dark brown, and slightly obliquely set. The body is strong, muscular, and not long; the tail is docked and carried at a slight angle away from the body. The coat is woolly but not soft and thick all over. In adult show Poodles, the Continental clip is normal. The alternative clip is the Dutch clip, a fairly close-cut body trim with baggy 'chaps' left on the legs.

Only solid colors are acceptable. The white Poodle should have dark eyes, black nose, lips, and toenails; the brown Poodle should have dark amber eyes, dark liver nose, lips, and toenails; and the blue Poodle should have dark eyes, lips, and toenails. The Standard Poodle is 15 inches and over at the shoulder.

Miniature Poodles and Toy Poodles are replicas in miniature of the Standard. The difference lies in the shoulder height, which for Miniatures should be under 15 inches and for Toys under 11 inches.

Top: Miniature Poodle.
Above: An apricot Toy Poodle.
Right: Pharaoh Hound.
Inset right: Pointer.

Pug *Britain*

The Pug probably takes its name from an old English word used as a term of endearment for pets – pet monkeys in particular. The breed is believed to have originated in China and was a smooth-coated cousin of the Pekingese. However, while over the years the Peke became longer, lower, and hairier, the Pug became taller, heavier, and smoother. It was imported into England from the Netherlands in the middle of the nineteenth century and quickly became popular.

The Pug has changed little since it came to Europe. It is a decidedly square and compact little dog – an extrovert in temperament. Its color is pure black, fawn, or silver with a black mask, black ears, and a black trace along the back. The weight varies between 14 and 18 pounds and the height at the shoulder should not exceed 13 inches.

Puli *Hungary*

The quaint little Puli, one of the four breeds of shepherd dogs in Hungary, is still a rarity in most countries. But when some Pulis were taken to the United States about 1930, its corded coat created a sensation and it has retained its popularity there.

Pulis are used in Hungary for hunting and as sheepdogs. In Germany some have been successfully trained for police work. But in the United States and Britain they are kept mainly as pets and companions.

The Puli is a medium-sized dog, its main characteristic being its corded coat, which is long and wavy with a tendency to tangle. The head appears almost round on account of the plentiful hair, the eyes are slightly slanted with a bright expression, and the ears are dropped. The tail is carried curled over the back.

The color may be black, gray, or white. The height at the shoulder is 17 to 19 inches for dogs, 16 to 18 inches for bitches.

Below left: Puli.
Below: Rhodesian Ridgebacks.

Rhodesian Ridgeback *South Africa*
The Rhodesian Ridgeback is now regarded as the national breed of South Africa. It is a strong, muscular, and active dog whose rough and vicious ancestors were used to hunt lions. The origins of the breed are unknown but it probably stems from crossbreeding between native African dogs and animals taken to Africa by the Europeans. The peculiarity of the breed is the ridge on the back, which is formed by the hair growing in the opposite direction to the rest of the coat. The ridge is normally clearly defined, tapering, and symmetrical – starting between the shoulders and continuing up to the hip bones. The Ridgeback's head is of moderate length and rather broad. The eyes are round and sparkling and the ears are carried close to the head. The coat is short, thick, and glossy. Color is light red wheaten, sometimes with a small white spot on the chest. The height at the shoulder for dogs is 25 to 27 inches, bitches 24 to 26 inches. The weight is about 80 pounds for dogs, 70 pounds for bitches.

Rottweiler *Germany*

The Rottweiler gets its name from the town of Rottweil in the Swabian Alps. The Rottweiler's ancestors were employed to herd cattle and as guard dogs. More recently they have been trained and employed as police dogs and war dogs.

The Rottweiler looks like a coarser and heavier version of the Dobermann but except for color and possibly temperament, the two breeds have little in common. If anything the Rottweiler is more docile and phlegmatic. The Rottweiler's stocky build does not prevent it from being agile. The head is fairly broad and rounded, the fore-face powerful, and the ears small and triangular in shape. The neck and body display strength and power. The tail is docked short and carried in line with the back. The coat is close and short, slightly longer on legs and tail.

The color is black with clearly defined tan markings. The weight is 80 to 90 pounds. The height at the shoulder 22 to 27 inches.

St. Bernard *Switzerland*

The large and handsome breed known as St. Bernard, or Great St. Bernard, is so-called because for centuries it has been bred at the Hospice of St. Bernard at the Great St. Bernard Pass in Switzerland. They were trained to track travelers lost in the snow. Nowadays the St. Bernard has found another purpose in life – as a pet. It is a big and heavy dog, but it has docile manners and is fairly easy to keep.

There are, in fact, two varieties of St. Bernard – smooth and rough-haired. The difference, as the names suggest, is only in the coat. In rough specimens this should be dense and flat and rather fuller around the neck. With the smooth variety it should be close and hound-like, slightly feathered on the thighs and tail. The St. Bernard is a large, heavy dog with a massive head and kindly, dark, rimmed eyes. The color is usually white and orange. The height at the shoulder for dogs is at least 28 inches, preferably more, and bitches slightly less.

Saluki *Arabia*

The Saluki, 'Arabian' or 'Gazelle' Hound is the oldest of the Greyhound varieties, and is unique in the canine world since for thousands of years it has remained pure and been kept from inter-breeding.

Since ancient times the Saluki has been the prized companion of the desert Bedouins, well adapted as it is for work as a hound in the dry, burning desert. In the West, the Saluki is kept almost exclusively as a pet. It moves very quickly and needs considerable exercise.

The body is lithe and graceful, the head finely chiselled and proudly carried. The coat is smooth and silky with long feathering on the ears and on the long, low-carried tail. Colors and sizes vary a great deal; dogs stand 23 to 28 inches at the

shoulder, while bitches are proportionately smaller.

There is also a smooth-coated variety of the Saluki which completely lacks feathering on ears and tail, but is in all other respects the same.

Samoyed *Arctic Siberia*

The Samoyed is a spitz breed which takes its name from a Siberian tribe called the Samoyedes. It was introduced to the West considerably earlier than other Arctic spitz breeds and was very popular even at the beginning of this century.

The typical show Samoyed is an affectionate and handsome creature, but full of action. It exudes serenity, power, and self-confidence. The head is powerful and wedge-shaped, the eyes almond-shaped and set well apart. The ears are erect and slightly rounded at the tips. The tail, not as tightly curled as in most other spitz breeds, is carried over the back when the dog is alert. The coat is very profuse, especially around the neck, on the tail, and on the feet.

The color is usually pure white, white and biscuit, or cream. The height at the shoulder is about 20 to 22 inches for dogs, 18 to 20 inches for bitches. The weight is 45 to 55 pounds for dogs, 36 to 45 pounds for bitches.

Top: Saluki.
Above: St Bernard.
Right: Samoyed.
Inset right: Schipperke.

Schipperke *Belgium*

The Schipperke's name is Belgian, and it has been translated as 'Little Boatman,' 'Little Captain,' and even 'Little Corporal.' The breed did not come into its own until about 100 years ago, but since then it has gained considerable popularity, although it is still not particularly common.

The Schipperke's main characteristics are lively temperament, a fox-like head with a pointed foreface, and stiffly erect ears. The eyes are small and dark brown, the body short and deep. It has no tail. The coat, which is close and rough, forms a thick ruff around the neck and 'trousers' on the thighs.

The color is usually black, but other whole colors are acceptable. The weight is up to 18 pounds. The height at the shoulder should not exceed 12 inches.

Schnauzer *Germany*

There are three varieties of Schnauzer – the Giant Schnauzer, the Standard Schnauzer, and the Miniature Schnauzer. The name comes from *schnauze*, meaning snout or muzzle, and the word *schnauzbart* is used to describe a moustache or a man with a moustache. And all three varieties of Schnauzer have conspicuous moustaches.

Although the Giant is virtually a bigger version of the Standard and Miniature, its forebears were sheepdogs and cattledogs in South Bavaria, subsequently mixed with other breeds. The Standard Schnauzer, on the other hand, is believed to have evolved from rough-coated dogs which were ratters – some say from crosses of the now extinct Schäferpudel and the Wire-haired German Pinscher. Both the Standard and the Miniature are outstanding ratters, but the Miniature is more than a dwarfed Standard. It was evolved from crosses of Standard Schnauzers with Affenpinschers.

Apart from size and weight requirements, the breed standard is the same for all three varieties of Schnauzer. All are clean-cut, powerful, square-built dogs with a temperament combining high spirits, reliability, endurance, and vigor. All have the characteristic moustache and beard, and all have tough, wiry, and dense coats. Colors are pure black or pepper and salt with a darker mark round the muzzle. Standard Schnauzer dogs stand about 19 inches at the shoulder, bitches 18 inches; Giant Schnauzers normally range from 21 to 25 inches, but some dogs reach 27 inches; with Miniature Schnauzers the height should not exceed 14 inches for dogs (13 inches for bitches).

Scottish Deerhound *Scotland*

It is believed that the ancestors of today's Scottish Deerhounds accompanied Phoenician traders to Britain, where eventually they became established in the Scottish Highlands. For a long time the Deerhound and the Irish Wolfhound were considered varieties of the same type of dog and the two breeds could not be properly distinguished. Today, however, they are easy to tell apart; even though the Deerhound may often be as tall as the Wolfhound, it is always considerably lighter and more graceful in build.

The Deerhound can perhaps more accurately be described as a wire-haired Greyhound. In temperament it is usually docile and friendly.

It is built on racy lines with a wiry, shaggy, blue-gray coat, dark eyes, small, thin, black ears, and a tail which almost reaches the ground. The height at the shoulder is at least 30 inches for dogs and at least 28 inches for bitches. The weight is 85 to 105 pounds and 65 to 80 pounds respectively.

Scottish Terrier *Britain*

The sturdy, thick-set little 'Scottie' has long been regarded as symbolically Scottish. Despite its small size and short legs, the Scottish Terrier is very active and surprisingly agile. The head is long, the nose large and black, and the deeply set eyes under the bushy eyebrows are extremely expressive. The coat is very coarse, thick, and wiry.

The color ranges from black, wheaten, brindle, iron gray, or grizzled, to sandy. The height at the shoulder is 10 inches, weight 18 to 22 pounds.

Sealyham Terrier *Britain*

In the middle of the nineteenth century, an eccentric sportsman (John Owen Tucker Edwardes) set out to breed terriers for hunting. Only the most vicious terriers were selected and crossed with various other breeds to produce dogs that were small and game, with the courage to stand up to fierce animals regardless of any disparity in size. Nowadays, although the present Sealyham is still hardy and obstinate, it has mellowed and has an astonishingly kindly temperament.

The Sealyham is an active, energetic, and strong dog. Despite its small size it is very heavily built and sturdy without appearing clumsy. The color is white, with or without lemon or brownish markings on the head and ears. The height at the shoulder should not exceed 12 inches. The weight for dogs is 20 pounds maximum, 18 pounds for bitches.

Left: Standard Schnauzers.
Right: Scottish Terrier.

Shih Tzu *Tibet*

Shih Tzu means 'lion dog' in Chinese, and the similarity between this breed and the Pekingese is so marked that it is obvious the Shih Tzu has been associated with China. Unlike the Pekingese, however, it has developed a very open and outgoing temperament.

The Shih Tzu is a very active, lively, and alert little dog with a very long, thick and straight coat. The hair is particularly abundant on the head and ears and grows upward on the nose, giving the head the typical 'chrysanthemum-like' effect. The muzzle is square and short but not wrinkled like a Pekingese.

All colors are acceptable, but a white blaze on the forehead and a white tip to the tail are highly prized. The height at the shoulder varies considerably, but is preferably just under 12 inches. The weight is up to 18 pounds – ideally 9 to 16 pounds.

Above: Scottish Deerhounds.
Above right: Siberian Husky.
Right: Sealyham Terrier.
Above far right: Shih Tzu.

Siberian Husky *USSR – Siberia*

The Siberian Husky is comparatively more 'civilized' and friendly toward man than other Arctic spitz breeds, and in consequence has assumed the role of companion and pet – a role rarely enjoyed by other sledge dogs until modern times. More recently he has been used in Alaska as a racer in sweepstake contests to track a snow-bound course, sometimes 400 miles long.

The Siberian Husky has a powerful and well-muscled body. His head is typical of the spitz, with erect ears and an alert expression, and the heavily haired tail is carried over the back in a sickle curve; when the dog is at rest, the tail is dropped. The coat is thick, fairly long, hangs loosely from the body, and is surprisingly soft.

All colors are acceptable. Most common is silver gray or tan with white markings. The height at the shoulder for dogs is 21 to 24 inches, 20 to 22 inches for bitches.

Silky Terrier *Australia*

The Australian Silky Terrier is not, as its name implies, a terrier at all but a member of the toy group. It emerged as the result of crosses between the Australian Terrier and various other terrier and toy dog varieties, including the Yorkshire Terrier which is responsible for two of the features separating the Australian Terrier from the Silky Terrier. These are the Silky Terrier's fairly long, thick, and silky coat, which is quite straight, and its body, which is more compact and shorter than the Australian Terrier's. (Mature dogs have a coat of 5 to 6 inches long from behind the ears to the base of the tail.) The Silky Terrier is slightly smaller than the Australian Terrier and stands about 9 inches at the shoulder. The color is blue and tan, but the blue may be silver blue, pigeon, or slate blue and the tan deep and rich.

Skye Terrier *Britain*

The Skye Terrier is a one-man dog, not vicious but distrustful of strangers. Originally it had much in common with the Scottish Terrier. The Skye Terrier is a heavily built dog with a long, low body, and at dog shows its long, straight coat flowing from a parting along the spine invariably attracts attention. The head is long with powerful jaws; the nose is black. The ears can be either pricked or dropped; the long tail is carried low and gracefully feathered. The color is blue gray, fawn, or cream with black points. The height at the shoulder is about 10 inches; the total length (nose to tip of tail) is about 41 inches; and weight averages about 25 pounds.

Soft-coated Wheaten Terrier *Eire*

The Soft-coated Wheaten Terrier is a native of Ireland, where it has been used for a variety of purposes ranging from driving cattle, guard dog, to ratter. The breed is a relative of both the Irish and Kerry Blue Terriers.

The Soft-coated Wheaten Terrier is a strong, active dog with a lovable disposition. It has a compact and short body without exaggerated features. The head is moderately long with small, well-fringed, thin ears folded forward. The eyes are dark with an intelligent expression and the whole body is covered with a profuse, soft coat — wavy or with large, loose curls.

The color is usually a light wheaten. The height at the shoulder is about 18 inches and the weight is 35 to 40 pounds.

Spinoni Italiani *Italy*

The Spinoni Italiani, or Spinone, is descended from the old European hunting dogs, the Griffons, which have contributed to the bloodlines of many modern gundog breeds.

In conformation, the Spinone is slightly heavier and coarser than the English Pointer. The head is large with a fairly broad and domed skull, the stop is not very accentuated, but the muzzle is well developed and square. The nose is brown, light brown, or liver with well-expanded nostrils. The ears are large and carried close to the head. The eyes, under bushy eyebrows, are light brown or yellow and they have an alert expression. The back is slightly arched over the loin and the chest is deep but not broad. The feet are round and the toes well knuckled up. The tail is carried in line with, or slightly above, the back. The coat is short, hard, and wiry.

The Spinone is either pure white, or white with small lemon or light brown markings. The height at the shoulder varies considerably, from 24 to 28 inches for dogs to 23 to 26 inches for bitches.

Staffordshire Bull Terrier *Britain*

The Staffordshire Bull Terrier is not one of the most popular terrier breeds, although it has a large following in its home country and in the United States. Such dogs are noted for their courage, intelligence, and tenacity. These qualities, coupled with affection for their friends — children in particular — make them all-purpose dogs. Originally they were used as guard and fighting dogs; nowadays they are mainly pets and companions.

The Staffordshire Bull Terrier is a smooth-coated dog which greatly resembles the Bull Terrier, although it does not have the latter's sweeping lines and head shape. It is a medium-sized, fairly long-legged terrier, heavily built and thick-set. The head is broad with a marked stop and half-pricked or 'rose' ears. The coat is short and glossy, and close to the skin.

The color ranges from particolor to brindle or whole-color in a variety of shades. The height at the shoulder is 14 to 16 inches. The weight for dogs is 28 to 38 pounds, bitches 24 to 34 pounds.

Below: Skye Terrier. Bottom left: Spinoni. Bottom: Staffordshire Bull Terrier. Right: Soft-coated Wheaten Terrier. Inset right: Sussex Spaniel.

Sussex Spaniel *Britain*
The massive and strongly built Sussex Spaniel is, unfortunately, becoming something of a rarity. As an established breed it has existed since the eighteenth century, having been evolved by crossing various existing spaniels. By the end of World War II, however, the number of dogs available for breeding had dropped to single figures, so to avoid too much inbreeding it was sometimes necessary to resort to outcrosses with other spaniels. The net result is that the number of true Sussex Spaniels has declined and it would seem that the breed is in danger of becoming extinct.

The Sussex Spaniel is an active, energetic, and strong dog who moves unlike any other spaniel with a characteristic roll. It is similar in conformation to the Clumber Spaniel but less heavy. Its eyes have a soft, slightly wistful expression and its ears are thicker than in most other spaniels. It has a long back and its legs are strong and muscular. The tail is docked but not too short, well feathered, and carried low. The coat is profuse and sleek with feathering on the legs, ears, and thighs.

The color is liver, shading to gold at the tips — a characteristic feature of the breed. The weight for dogs is about 45 pounds. The height at the shoulder is 15 to 16 inches.

Tibetan Spaniel *Tibet*

The little Tibetan Spaniel is a toy dog breed descended from the temple dogs of ancient Tibet and it is fairly rare. 'Spaniel,' of course, has a modern European flavor – originally all 'spaniels' were gundogs, but the name was given later to a few toy breeds which bore some resemblance to the spaniel proper. However, the Tibetan Spaniel is not related in any way to spaniels; it can perhaps be described best as something between a Pekingese and a Shih Tzu.

It is an elegant little creature with a slightly domed head that is small in proportion to its body. Its ears are dropped like those of the Pekingese, but the eyes are not as large and prominent and the legs are longer and straighter. The tail is carried in a plume over the back and the coat is less profuse than that of the Pekingese.

Many colors are acceptable: white, cream, fawn, golden, brown, or black – whole-colors or particolors. The height at the shoulder for dogs should not exceed 11 inches or about 9 inches for bitches.

Tibetan Terrier *Tibet*

The Tibetan Terrier comes from Tibet, but it is certainly not a true terrier as it was not bred to go to ground. For this reason it is classed as one of the non-sporting dogs. However, like all terriers, the Tibetan Terrier has an alert and intelligent temperament; it is neither fierce nor pugnacious.

In general appearance it is not unlike an Old English Sheepdog in miniature. Its head has a marked stop, a black nose, large dark eyes, and vee-shaped pendant ears. Its coat, which is profuse and either straight or wavy, is particularly abundant on the head. Its tail is of medium length, very well feathered, and carried in a gay curl over the back.

The color is usually white, gray, cream, or black, but may vary considerably. The height at the shoulder is 14 to 16 inches.

Vizsla *Hungary*

The Vizsla is Hungary's most famous hunting dog. It is of general pointer type and comes in two varieties – Short-haired and Wire-haired. Of the two, the Short-haired variety is the more common and better known in countries other than Hungary; its main characteristic is probably the color of its coat – a 'rusty gold.' Also characteristic is the pale, liver-colored nose; the eyes are medium size and brown. In general conformation the Vizsla is more robust and less refined than the pointer, its head is coarser with larger ears and the tail is docked. In temperament it is lively, affectionate, and easy to train. Apart from rusty gold, the color may also be a sandy yellow in varying shades. The height at the shoulder is 22 to 24 inches for dogs, 21 to 23 inches for bitches.

The Wire-haired Vizsla was evolved by crossing Short-haired Vizslas with German Wire-haired Pointers. This breed is slightly bigger than the Short-haired variety, otherwise the only distinguishing feature is the texture of the coat which is rough and forms whiskers on the chin.

Above: Hungarian Vizsla.
Below: Tibetan Spaniels.
Right: Weimaraner.

Weimaraner *Germany*

The Weimaraner is the most senior of the German sporting dogs. It is a medium-sized, gray dog with a head rather like that of a pointer and light-colored eyes – in shades of amber, gray, or blue-gray. The Weimaraner's head is moderately long and aristocratic, but the lobular ears are larger and longer than those of the pointer and they are set high. The body is well developed and muscular, presenting a general appearance of power, stamina, alertness, and balance. There are Short-haired, Wire-haired, and Long-haired Weimaraners, but the Short-haired variety is the most common. The tail of the two former varieties is docked two-thirds from the root, while only the tip of the tail of the Long-haired type is removed.

The color varies from mouse gray to silver gray with lighter shades on the head and ears. The nose is gray, the lips and gums pinkish. The height at the shoulder is 23 to 25 inches for dogs, 22 to 24 inches for bitches.

Welsh Corgi, Cardigan *Britain*

Corgi is the old Celtic word for dog. It is not generally appreciated that there are two varieties: one, the Cardigan Corgi, is not especially common even in its home country; the other variety, the Pembroke, is the one that most people are referring to when they speak of the Welsh Corgi.

The Cardigan Corgi is slightly bigger and heavier than the Pembroke and it is usually considered to have a calmer and quieter temperament. The head is moderately broad but foxy and the ears are larger and more rounded than those of the Pembroke. The tail is fairly long, resembling a fox brush, and set in line with the body – not curled over the back.

All colors except pure white are acceptable, but red or brindle with white markings, or blue merle, are most popular. The height at the shoulder is approximately 12 inches for a dog.

Welsh Corgi, Pembroke *Britain*

The Pembroke Welsh Corgi is the only British spitz. It is a sturdy, low-set, alert, and active dog with an intelligent and bold expression – slightly fox-like in appearance. Its head is carried proudly and its ears are medium-sized and slightly pointed. The body is rather long with a level back and short, heavily boned, straight legs. The tail is usually short by nature. The coat is of medium length and dense, not wiry. The color ranges from sable red to tricolor with white markings on legs, neck, and muzzle. The height at the shoulder is 10 to 12 inches, weight about 20 to 24 pounds.

Welsh Springer Spaniel *Britain*

The 'Welsh Spaniel' or 'Springer,' which is of very ancient and pure origin, was bred and preserved purely for working purposes. For 200 years or so it has remained practically free of foreign blood; nevertheless it does resemble the English Springer Spaniel.

The Welsh Springer is a spirited, compact, and very active dog, obviously built for endurance and hard work. The head, which is neither short not chubby, differs from that of the English Springer in that it has shorter ears. The eyes are hazel or dark brown, the nose flesh-colored or black. The body is strong and muscular, the feet small and cat-like, and the tail is low-set and carried low. The coat is smooth, thick, and silky but not too profuse and with moderate feathering on the ears and back of the legs.

The color is always white with dark rich-red markings. The weight is about 35 to 45 pounds and height at shoulder about 16 inches.

Far left: Welsh Terrier.
Left: Welsh Springer Spaniel.
Below: Cardigan Corgi.
Right: Pembroke Corgis.

Welsh Terrier *Britain*

The Welsh terrier could be said to be a sort of miniature Airedale, looking very much like a Fox Terrier and with Fox Terrier characteristics. It is a fearless little dog, affectionate, obedient, and easily controlled — qualities that make him an eminently suitable dog for town life. Furthermore, Welsh Terriers are normally of a hardy and robust constitution and need no pampering. They are easy to train and anxious to please.

The head of a Welsh Terrier is flatter and rather wider between the ears than the Wirehaired Fox Terrier, giving it more of a masculine appearance. The coat is coarse and wiry and the color is black and tan or black grizzle and tan. The height at the shoulder should not exceed 15½ inches, and 20 to 21 pounds is considered to be the average weight.

West Highland White Terrier *Britain*

Scotland has five main breeds of terriers — Cairns, Dandie Dinmonts, Skyes, Scottish Terriers, and West Highland Whites — and the Cairn is probably the oldest and still the most popular. But in recent years the West Highland White has been steadily climbing the popularity ladder. It is a hardy breed but it has a friendly disposition and makes an ideal companion. It is a natural working dog and is fearless and persistent in chasing its prey.

The general appearance of the West Highland is that of a small, hardy-looking terrier. It has a short, compact body similar to that of the Scottish Terrier. However, the West Highland is not as low-set as the Scottie, nor is the head as long and, because of its abundant coat, the West Highland's skull appears to be completely round. The eyes are set wide apart and are sunk slightly into the head; the nose is black. The ears are small, pointed, and carried stiffly erect. The coat is profuse, about 2 inches long, straight, and hard except on the ears where it is smooth and vevelty. The color is pure white and height at the shoulder is about 11 inches.

Above: Whippets.
Left: Yorkshire Terrier.

Whippet *Britain*

The Whippet probably descended from small greyhounds and various types of terriers, and it was even used early in its history for racing and rabbiting. In some Whippets the lively terrier blood is still apparent, while others have the quiet disposition typical of the Greyhound.

In conformation the Whippet is a smaller version of the Greyhound but with a slightly sturdier frame. The head is long and lean, the jaws powerful, and the eyes dark. The ears are fine in texture, with the tips folded when the dog is alert. The back is slightly arched over the loin with well-defined flanks. All in all it is a dog which gives a general impression of balanced muscular power combined with great elegance.

Fawn, brindle, and white in various combinations are the most common colors, but any color or mixture of colors is acceptable. The height at the shoulder is just over 18 inches for dogs and about 17 inches for bitches.

Wire-haired Pointing Griffon *France*

The Wire-haired Pointing Griffon is a somewhat slow-working pointing dog and retriever with an excellent nose. It is a heavily built, longish-legged dog. The head is long and narrow, the eyes large and amber or light brown. The ears are set high, carried dropped, of medium size, and sparsely coated. The nose is always brown. The body and legs are strong and muscular, and the tail docked to about one-third of its length and carried in line with the back or slightly above it. The coat is rough and shaggy without curl which gives the dog an ungroomed look.

The color is steel gray or light gray with chestnut-colored patches. The height at the shoulder for dogs is about 22 inches, and 20 inches for bitches.

Yorkshire Terrier *Britain*

The Yorkshire Terrier is an attractive, long-coated toy breed which has retained the lively terrier temperament of its older relatives. As a recognized breed, the Yorkshire Terrier is of fairly recent origin, having evolved during the nineteenth century through attempts to create a new toy dog. At one time the size of the dog and the length of its coat were considered of prime importance but now, fortunately, emphasis is also placed on soundness and a bright temperament.

The coat should be long enough to reach the ground. The steel blue color of the body coat should be pure and not intermingled with the tan markings on the head, chest, and legs. The weight should not exceed 7 pounds, while the height at the shoulder is about 8 inches.